Shelley Heffler

Selected Artworks
2013 - 2017

Published by
Shelley Heffler

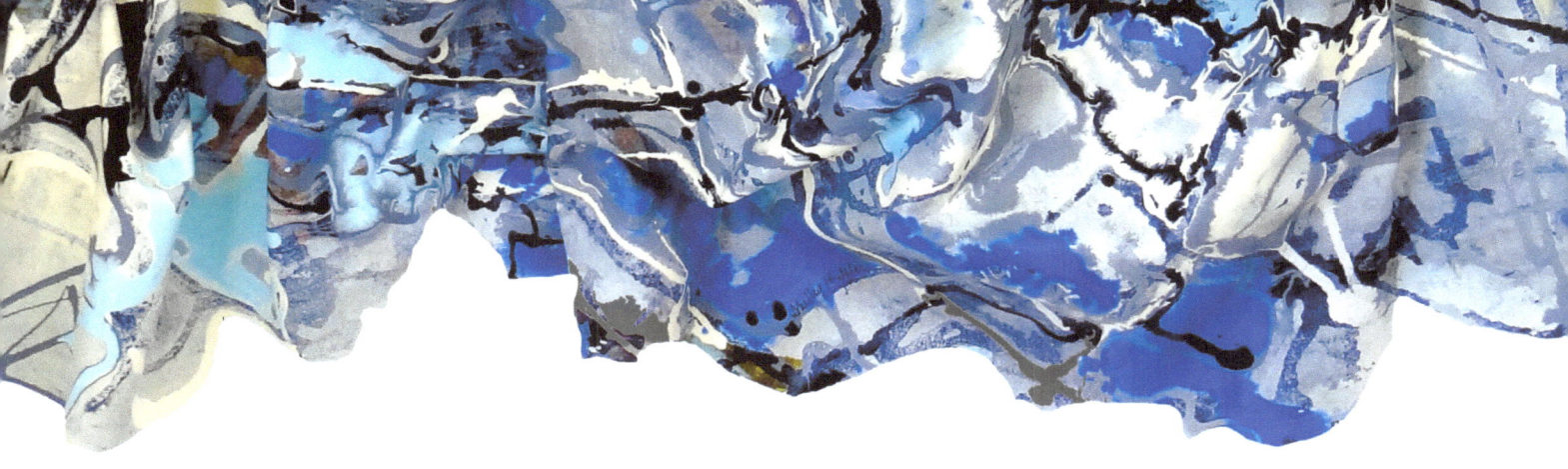

Artist Statement

Every day the flux of physical as well as cyber mobility has had an impact on human experience. I think about society in a networked, complex and spatially expanded way that includes concepts of boundaries and connectivity. Even though everything seems to be a part of world systemic processes and global networks, the notion of place and location remains temporal and mutable.

Cartography and abstraction are two languages used in my work. I am interested in engaging the viewer on a journey that preexists language and generates ideas and messages that relate to the viewer personally and metaphorically. The works explore global concerns and shifting boundaries of society and politics. Imagery is derived from a variety of resources such as transit systems, ancient ruins, floor plans, city grids, topography and geography; time and space coexist in a compressed world. I strive to reinvent or mutate natural and artificial spatial relationships that exist on the earth's surface, and to that end, open a dialog for cultural and global issues.

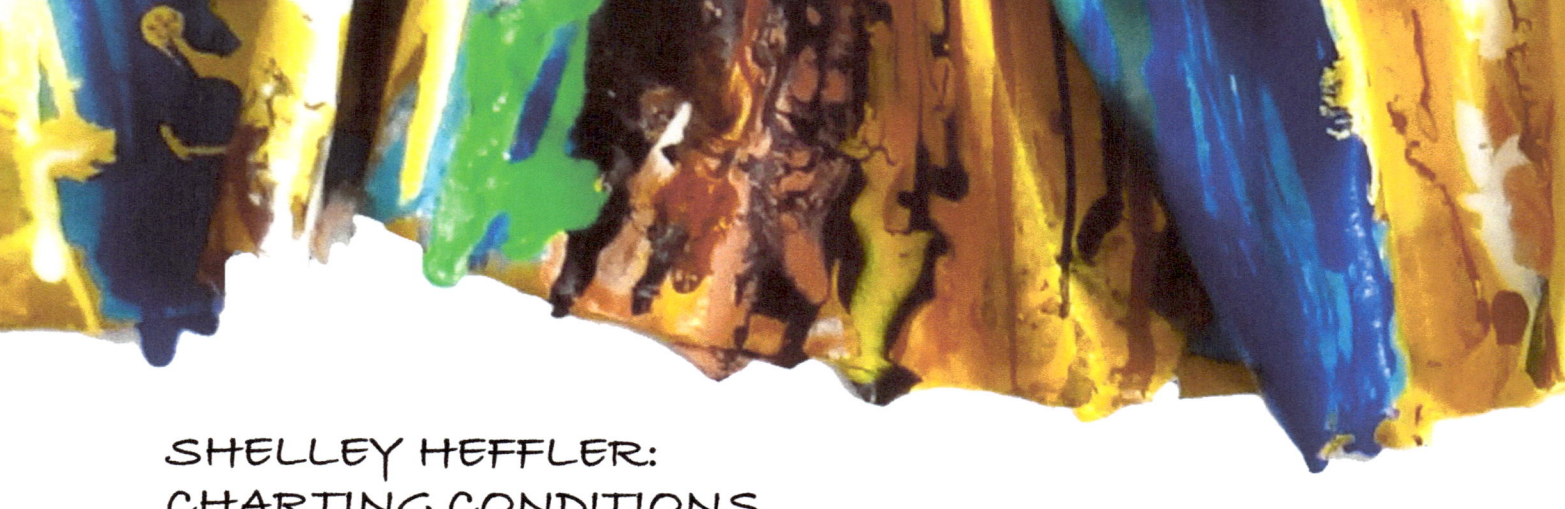

SHELLEY HEFFLER: CHARTING CONDITIONS

By Peter Frank

"…The notion of place and location remains temporal and mutable," writes Shelley Heffler, giving context to her engagement of maps – and the process of mapping – in her work. Like so many artists, Heffler has responded deeply to the aesthetic pleasures of cartography, and has made maps, mapping, and the qualities of charting ground and situation a central aspect of her work. Unlike so many artists – certainly painters – Heffler has taken up the making and the consideration of maps as much as a signal to the world as a celebration of it.

To be sure, many artists who engage maps are concerned, even preoccupied, with the declining condition of the terrestrial environment. For the most part, however, they employ maps as supportive documents, or at most icons of information – notational stand-ins for the real spaces they chart – so that the visual particulars of the maps presented recede into the presentation of information. Heffler, committed to painting and to a personalized, even internalized notion of abstraction, brings forward those particulars. Or, rather, she brings forward the condition of such particularity, making her work a place where her impulse to abstraction meets the factuality of cartography. Impulse and factuality both are bolstered in her art by the additional fact that the process of translating place and location to corresponding marks on a plane is itself a process of abstraction.

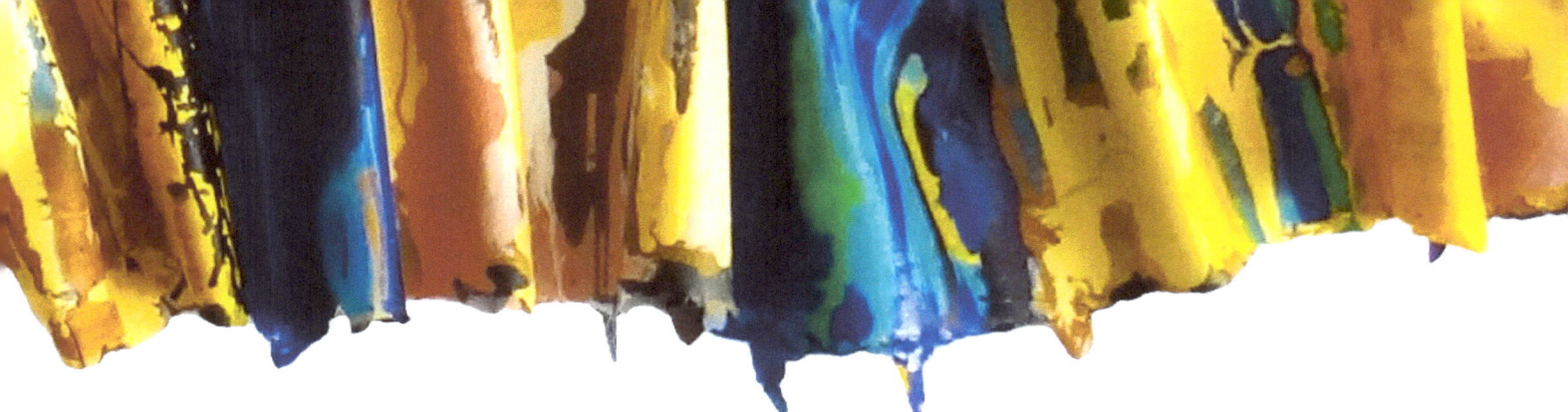

A crucial part of Heffler's approach is to give heft and texture, not just line and color, to her invented maps. A good portion of her work – notably the "Altered Hybrid" paintings – consists as much of three-dimensional construction as it does of two-dimensional rendition. And even the physically flat paintings, most recently the "Maps of the Imagination" and "Anthropocene Art," infer a material presence as much off as on the canvas. The Anthropocene works conjure a vivid topography, as much by the cartography-like inscriptions Heffler has imposed on them as by the articulated grounds – mountainous or effluvial, according to the palette and the movement of pigment – at their base. The "Maps of the Imagination," by contrast, strongly suggest urban densities, webbed as they are with lines inscribed as much according to underlying grids as to the flow of paint. The Anthropocene artworks infer the imprint humans make on the earth; the Maps of the Imagination infer the accretion of imprints humans make on themselves.

Shelley Heffler's evocation of ecological unease is just that, an evocation. It asks us to look at what we are doing to our surroundings – and thus ourselves – by communicating through abstract gesture, however carefully calibrated, the depth and persistence of our insult. The agitation of Heffler's painterly touch does not simply bespeak her own angst in the face of climate change, but brings to immediate awareness a sense of environmental degradation, almost as if that degradation were playing itself out on the canvas, before our eyes. By the same token, the gravity of Heffler's work calls attention to the work itself as art; these paintings are graphically, coloristically, and texturally compelling as paintings, their coarse and furious beauty never far from the surface. It is, finally, the earth's beauty shining through – and the matching beauty of hope, hope that humankind's wisdom can overtake its profligacy.

May 2017
Aschaffenburg, Germany

Anthropocene Paintings

The Anthropocene describes the geologic epoch where humans have impacted and altered the Earth's systems. This body of work is inspired by how we use and interpret our planet, chronicling the visible scars and manipulations of the earth as seen from above. Examining the human role in shaping our current geological era, the work questions the impulse to alter the Earth's story through the rearrangement of past accumulations of our actions.

Above, Below and Beyond # I

acrylic on canvas
30"x40"

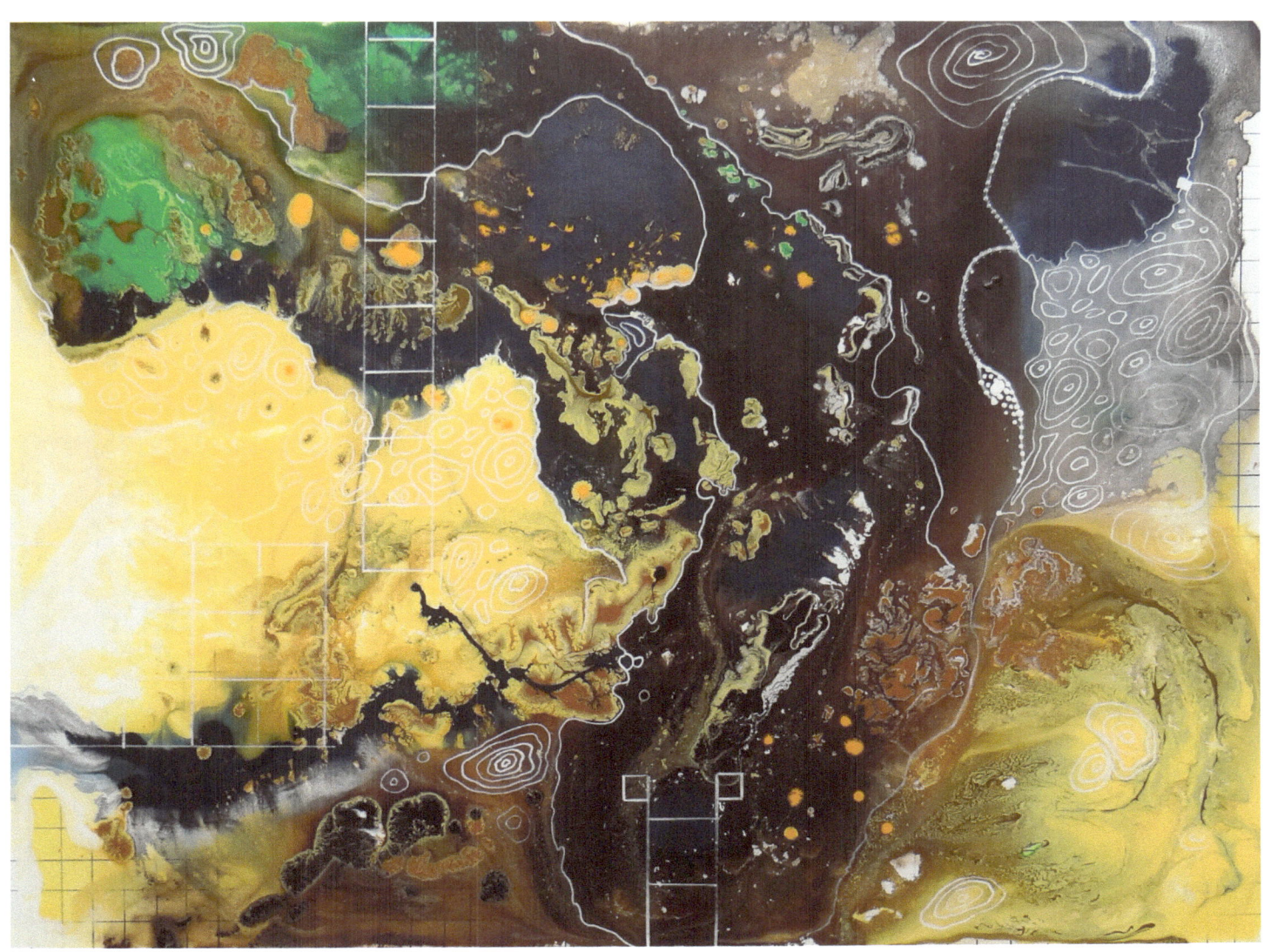

Above, Below and Beyond #2

acrylic on canvas
30"x40"

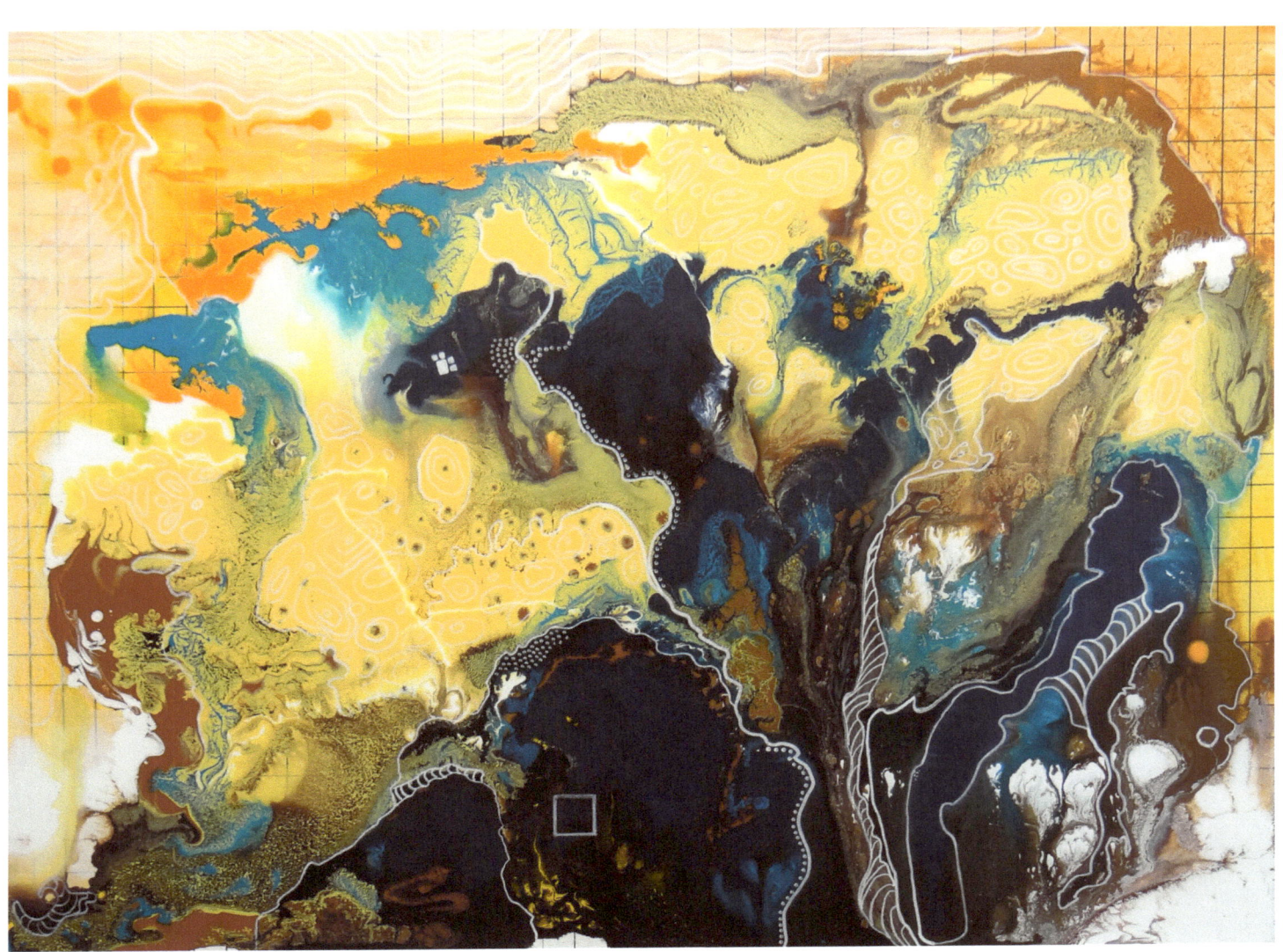

History of Abandonment

acrylic on canvas
24"x36"

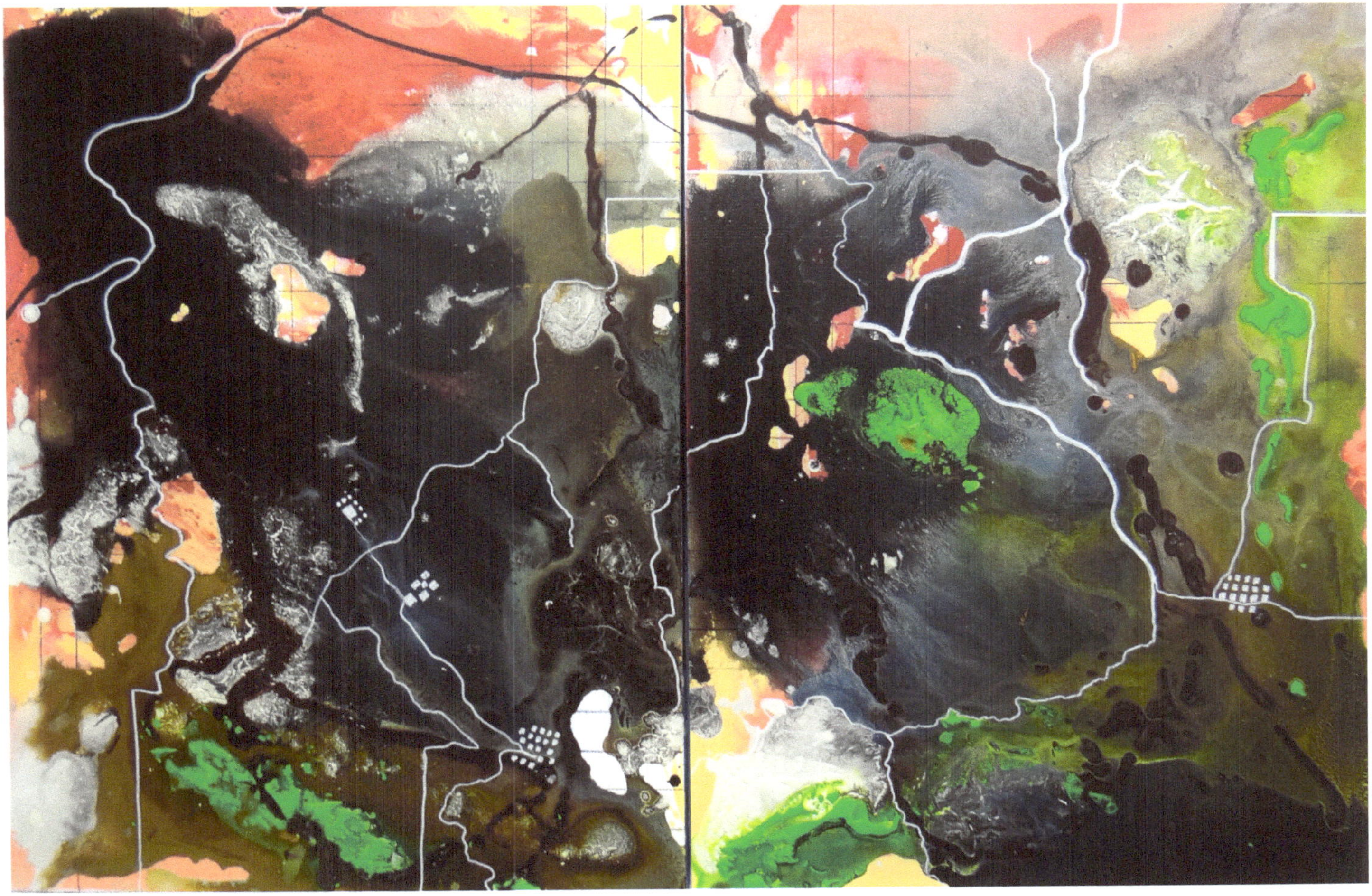

The Journey #1, #2, #3

acrylic on canvas
30"x15"

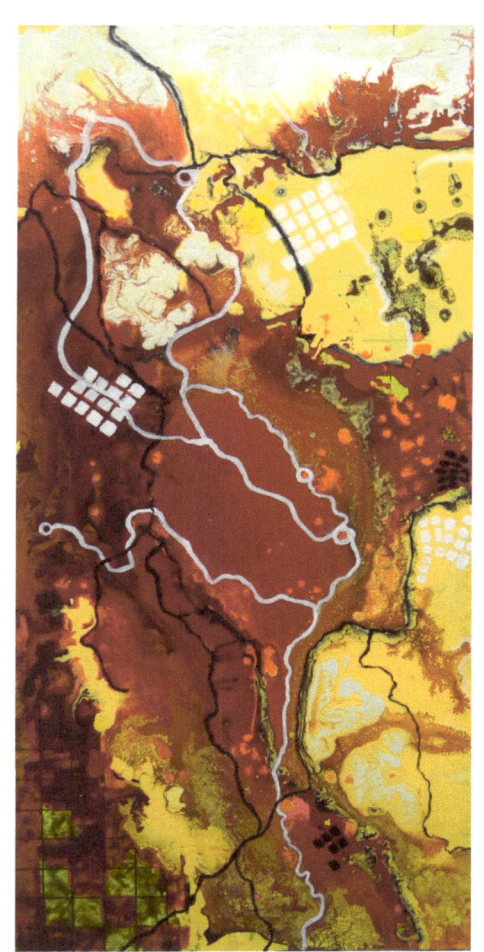
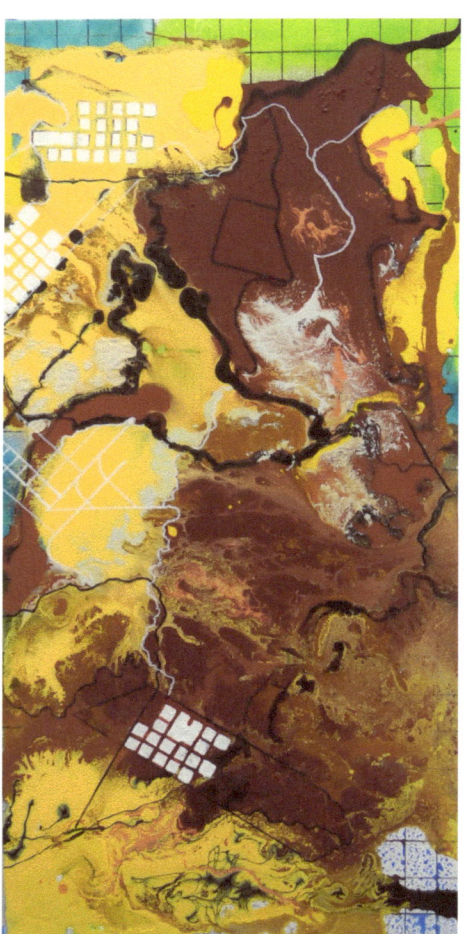
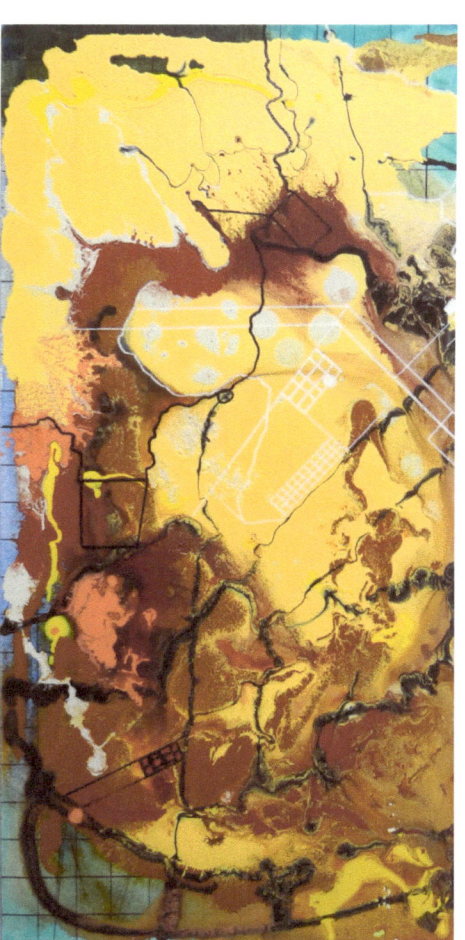

30 Miles Stretch

acrylic on canvas
40"x32"

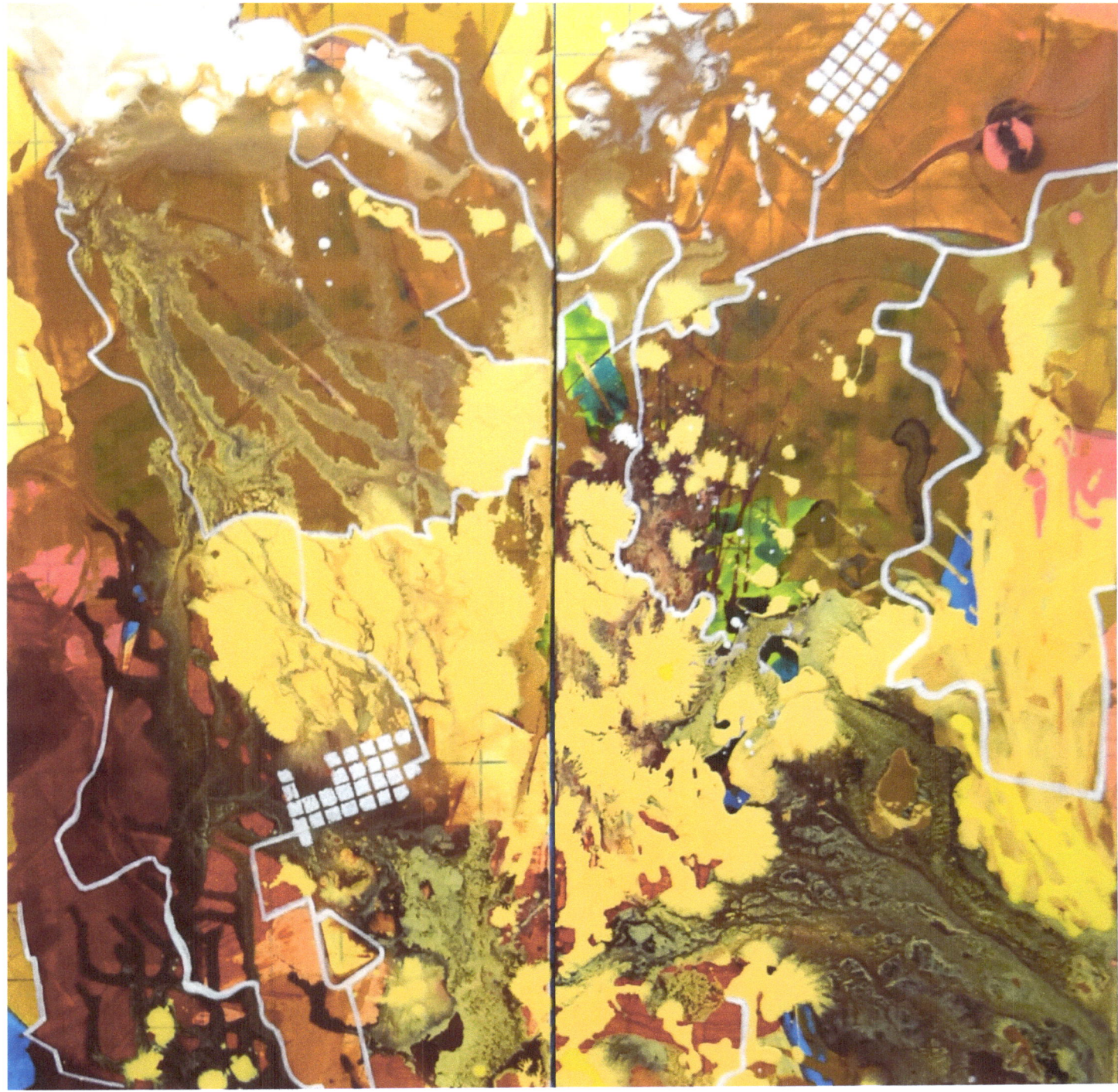

Judgement Day

acrylic on canvas
48"x58"

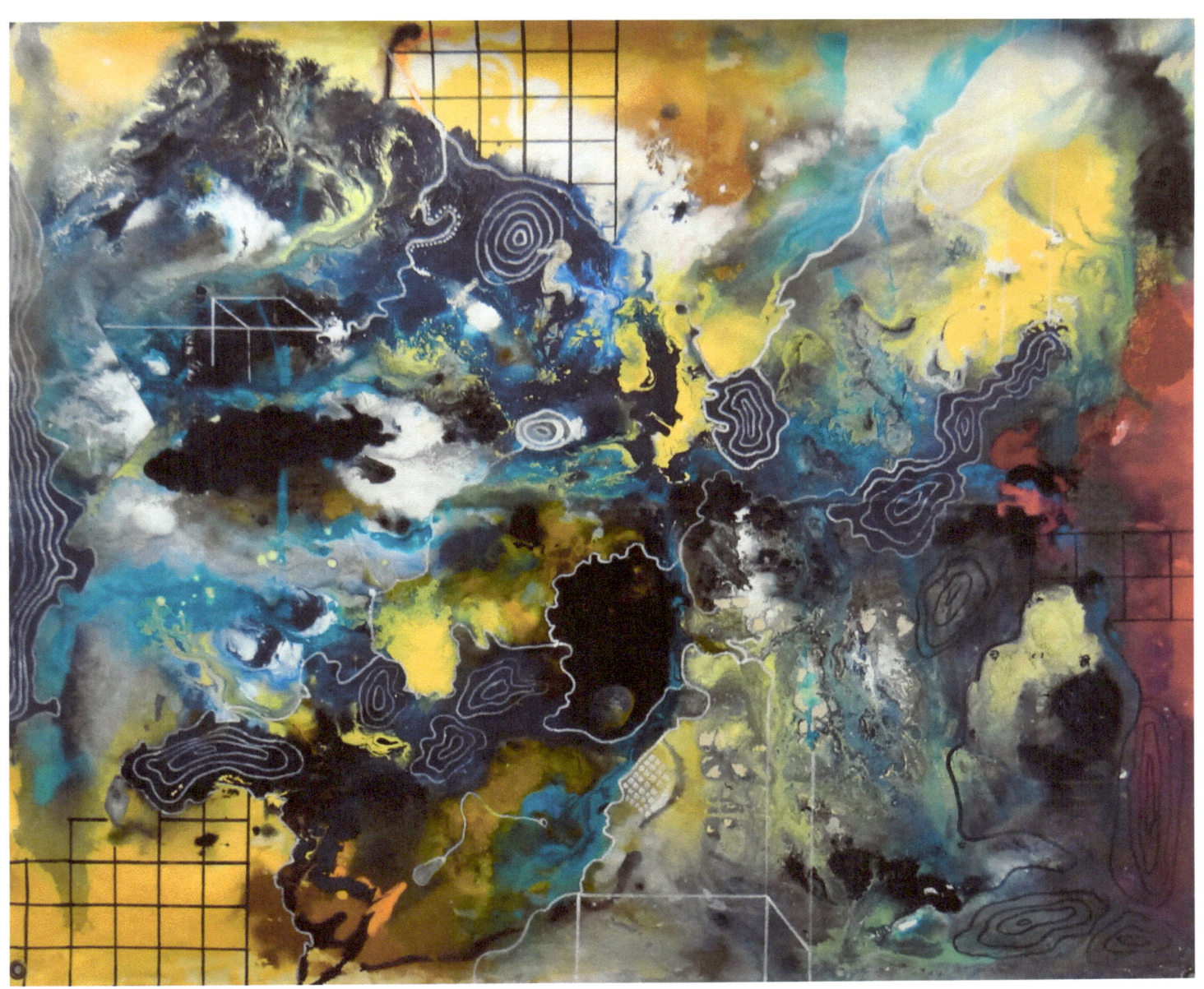

Subterranean Homesick Blues #2

acrylic on canvas
40"x40"

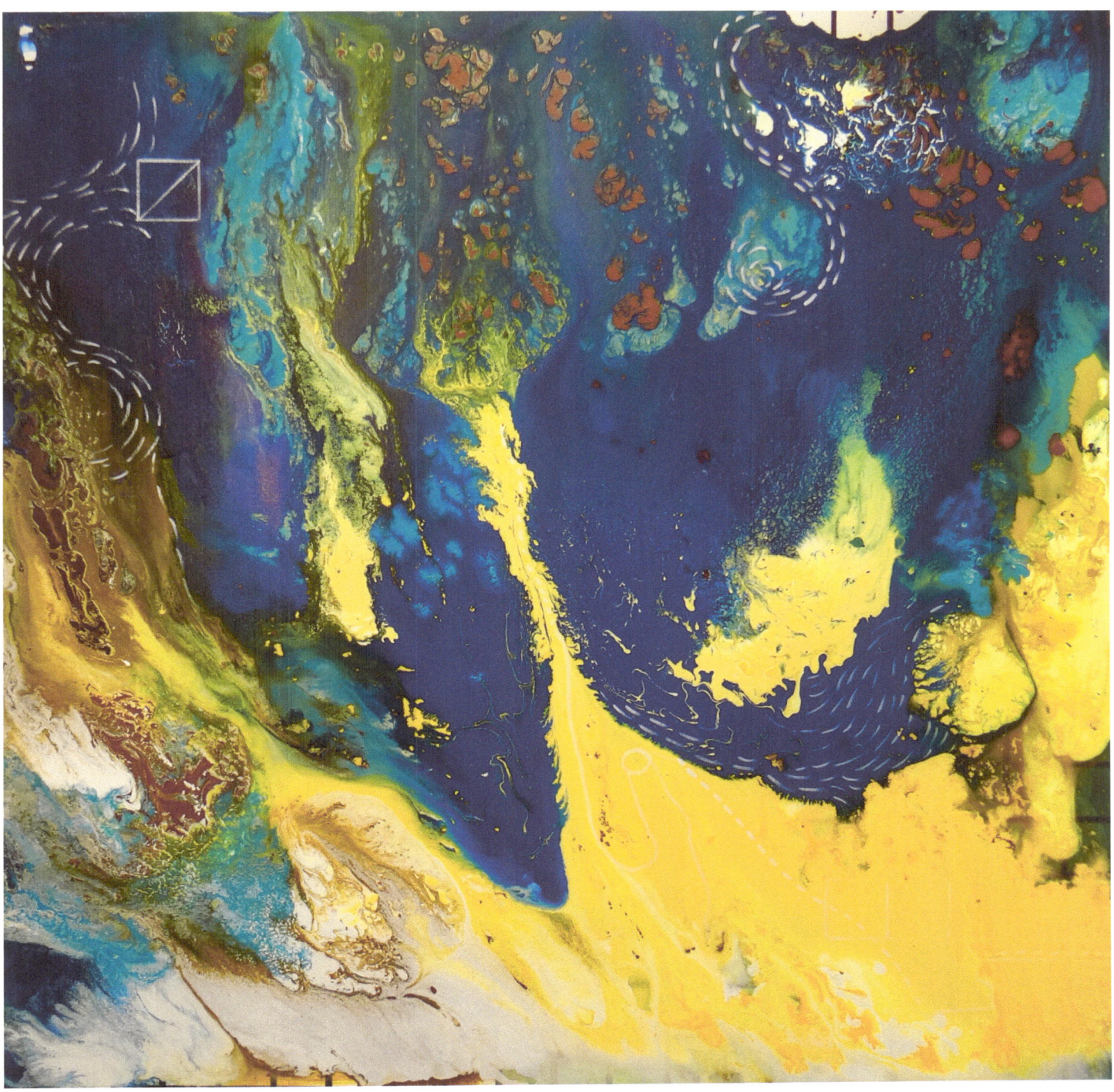

Subterranean Homesick Blues #3

acrylic on canvas
40"x40"

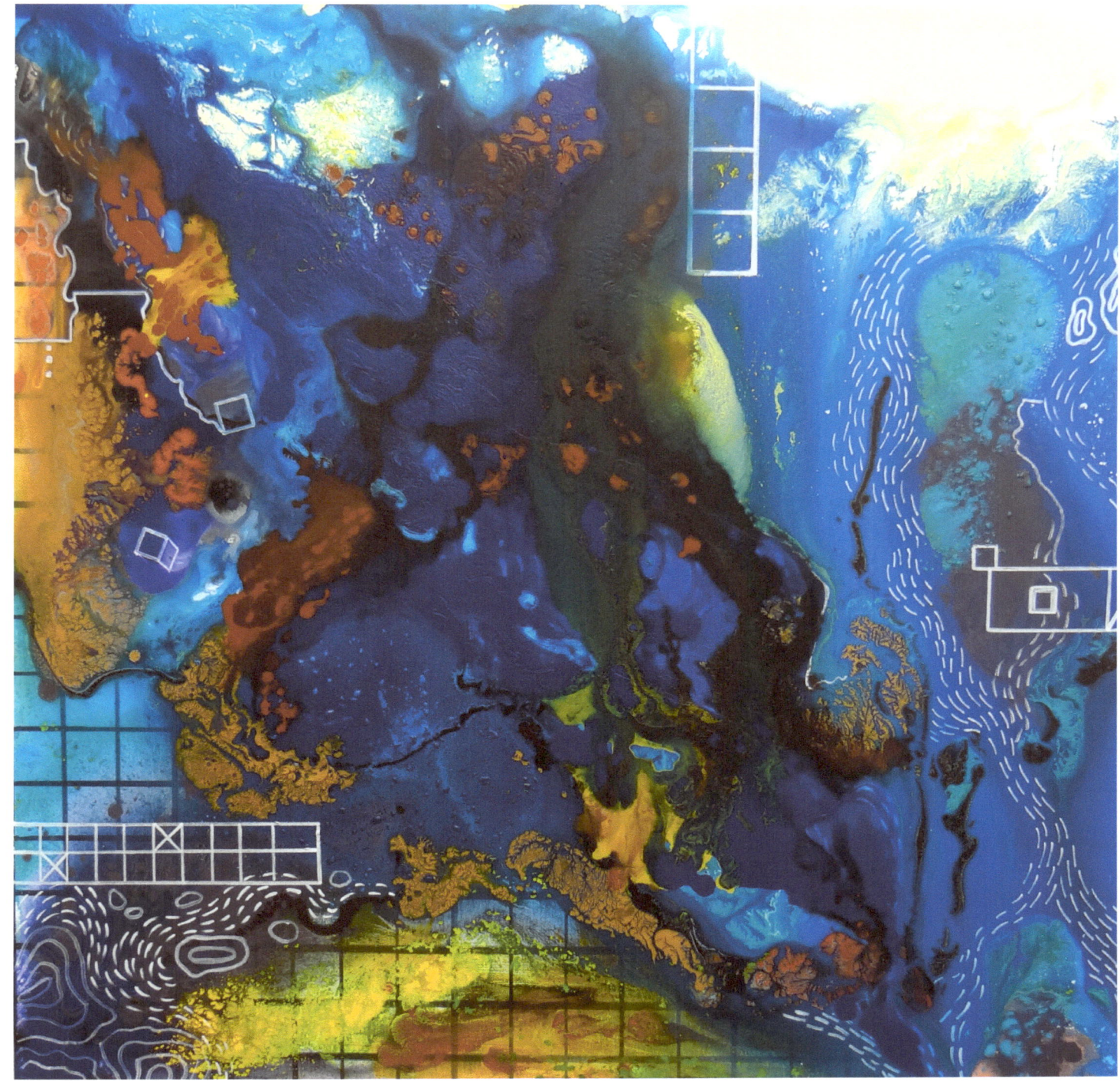

After the Fall #1, #2, #3

acrylic on canvas
24"x20"

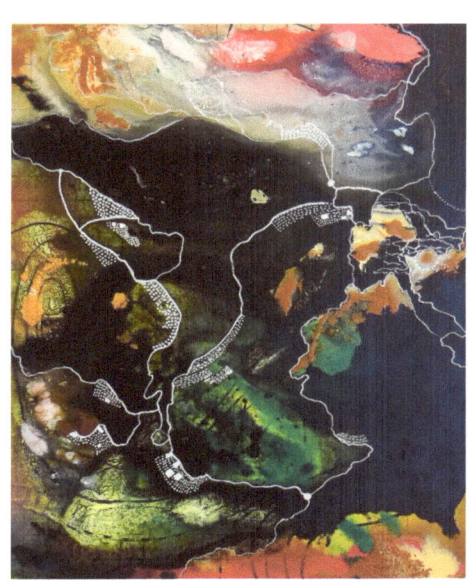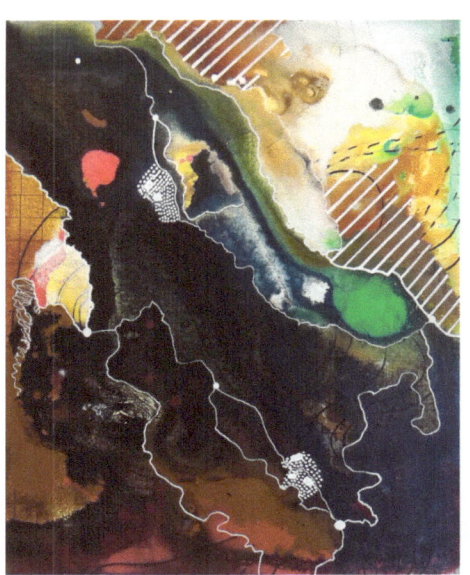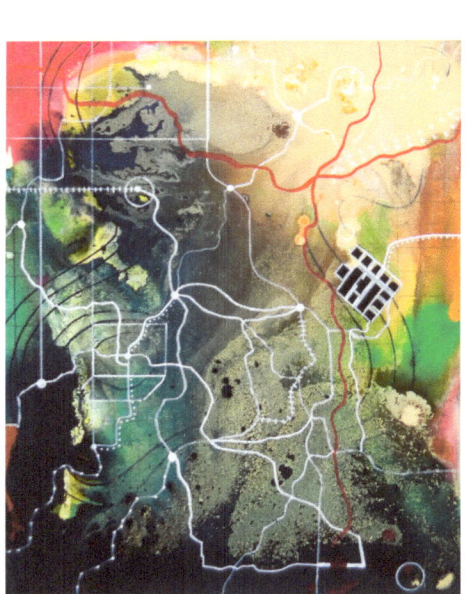

Altered Hybrid Paintings

My practice is concerned with the traditional language of painting and the formal relationships of the pictorial surface. I am interested in the materiality of paint, particularly the plasticity of acrylic paint and its malleable properties. Through stages of experimentation, I've explored ways in which to manipulate painting from its traditional 2-dimensional support and bring it out into the viewer's sphere.

A Road Less Traveled

acrylic on canvas
28"x36"x4"

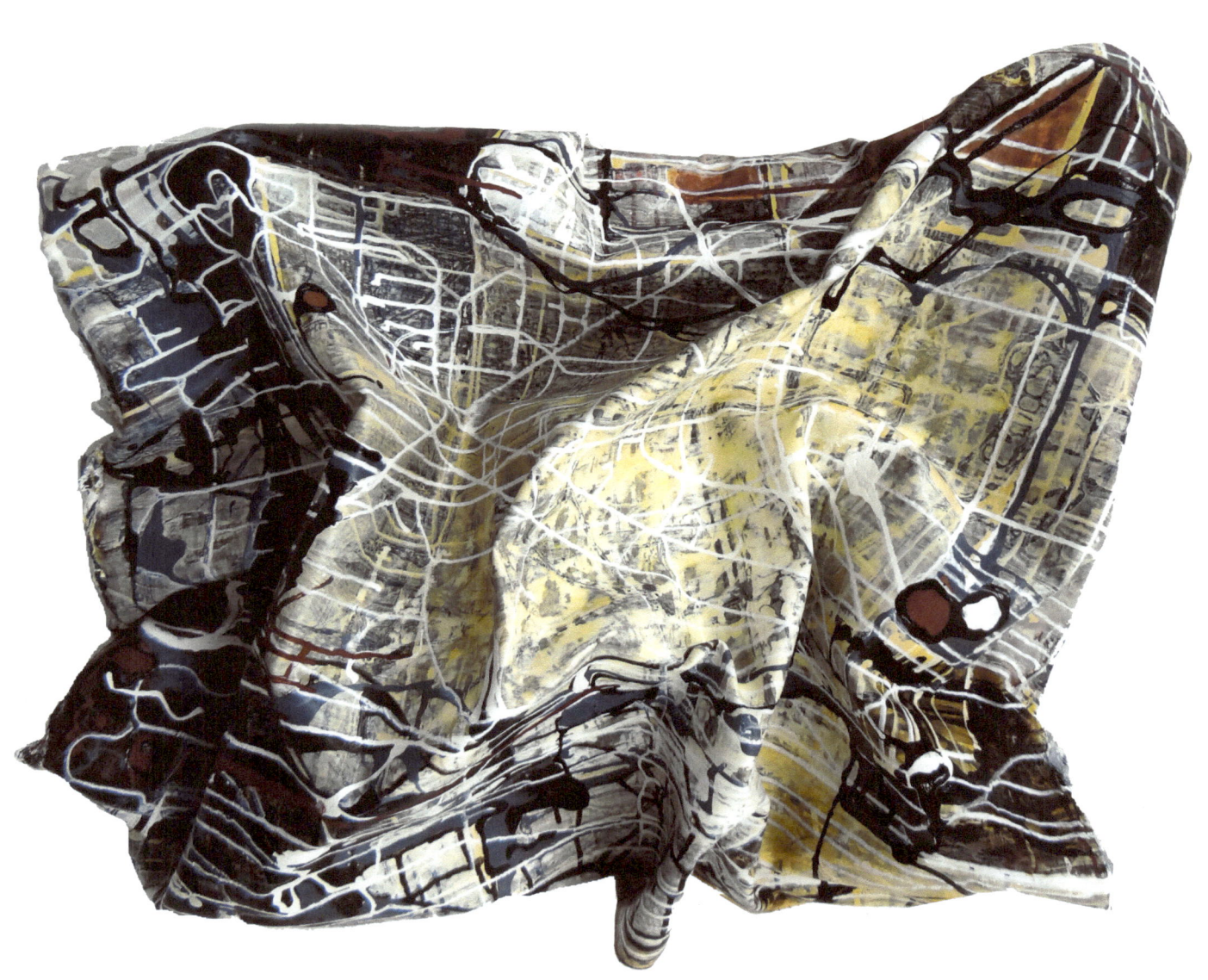

Cracked

acrylic on canvas
36"x48"x5"

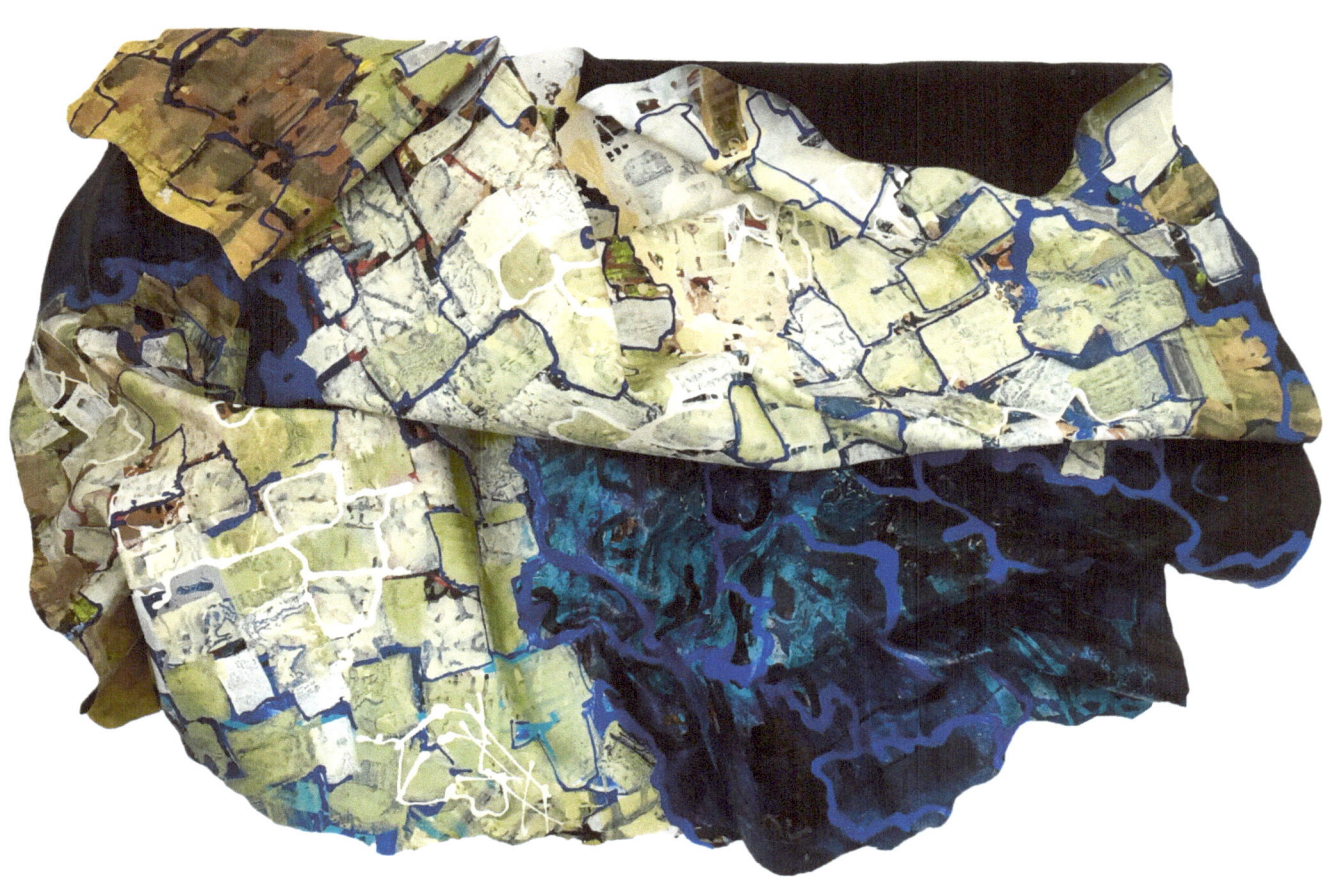

Silver Lining

acrylic on canvas
36"x48"x5"

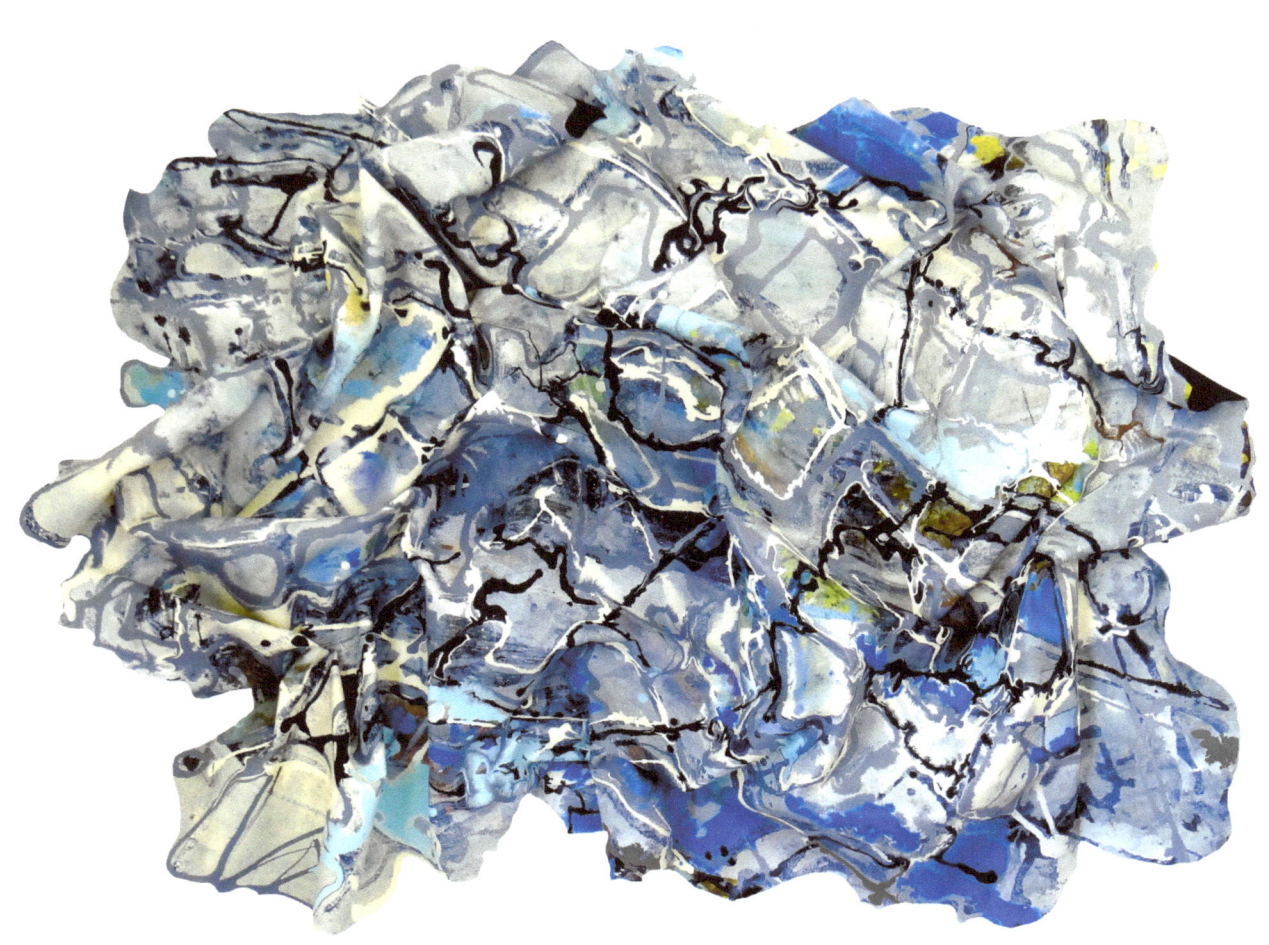

Starry Night

acrylic on canvas
42"x36"x8"

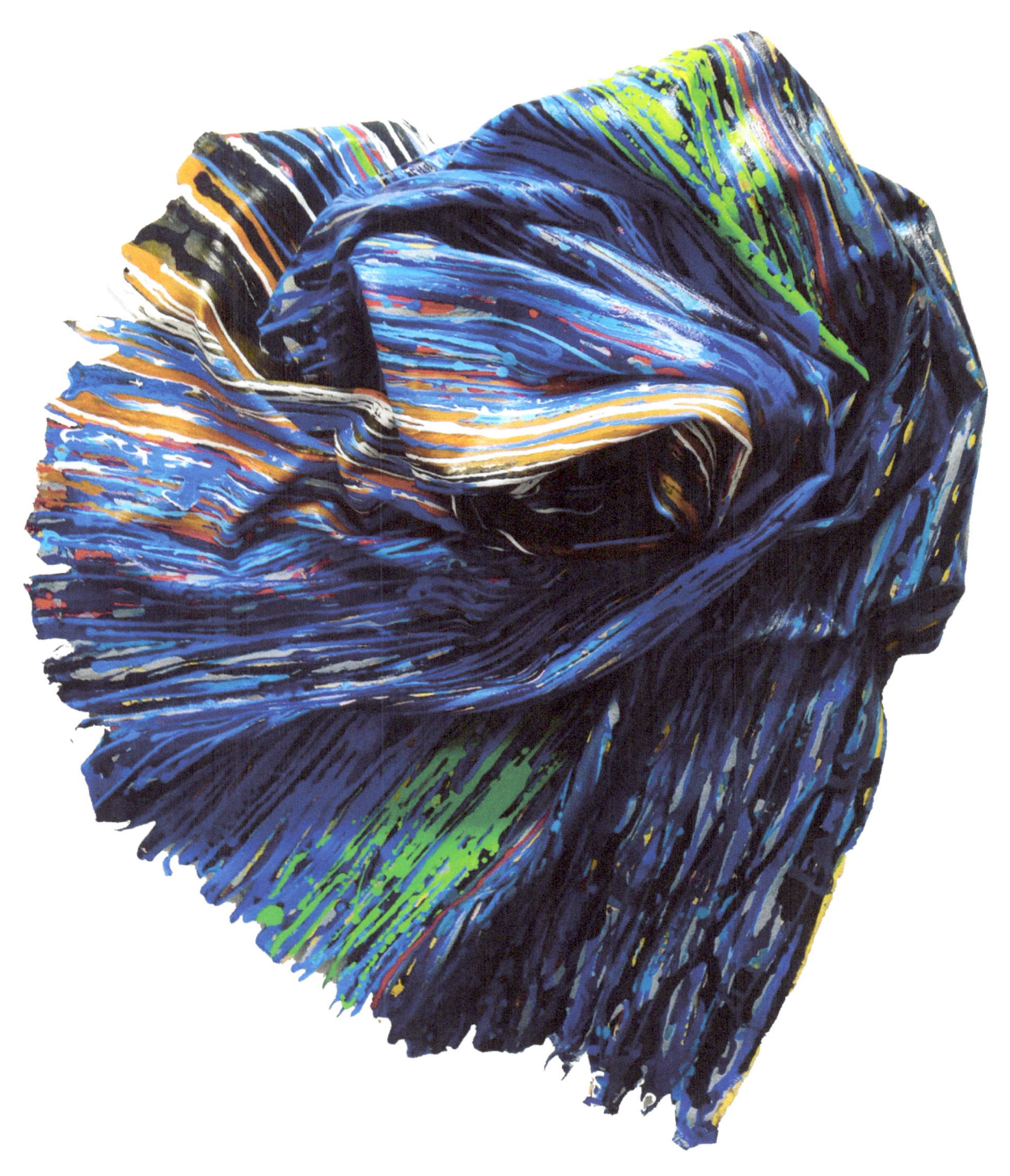

Red Hurricane

acrylic on canvas
36"x36"x4"

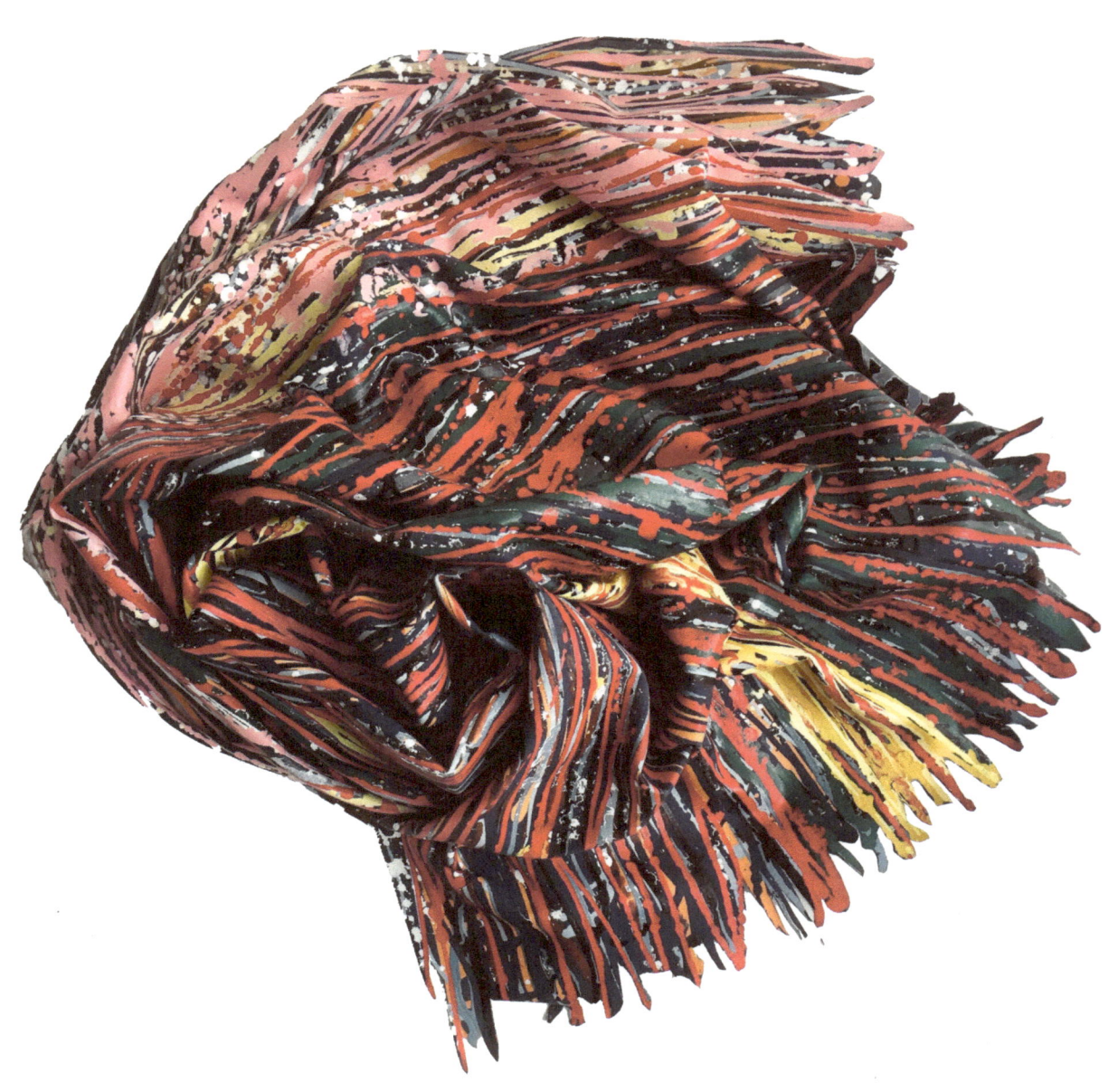

Urban Decay

acrylic on canvas
42"x24"x12"

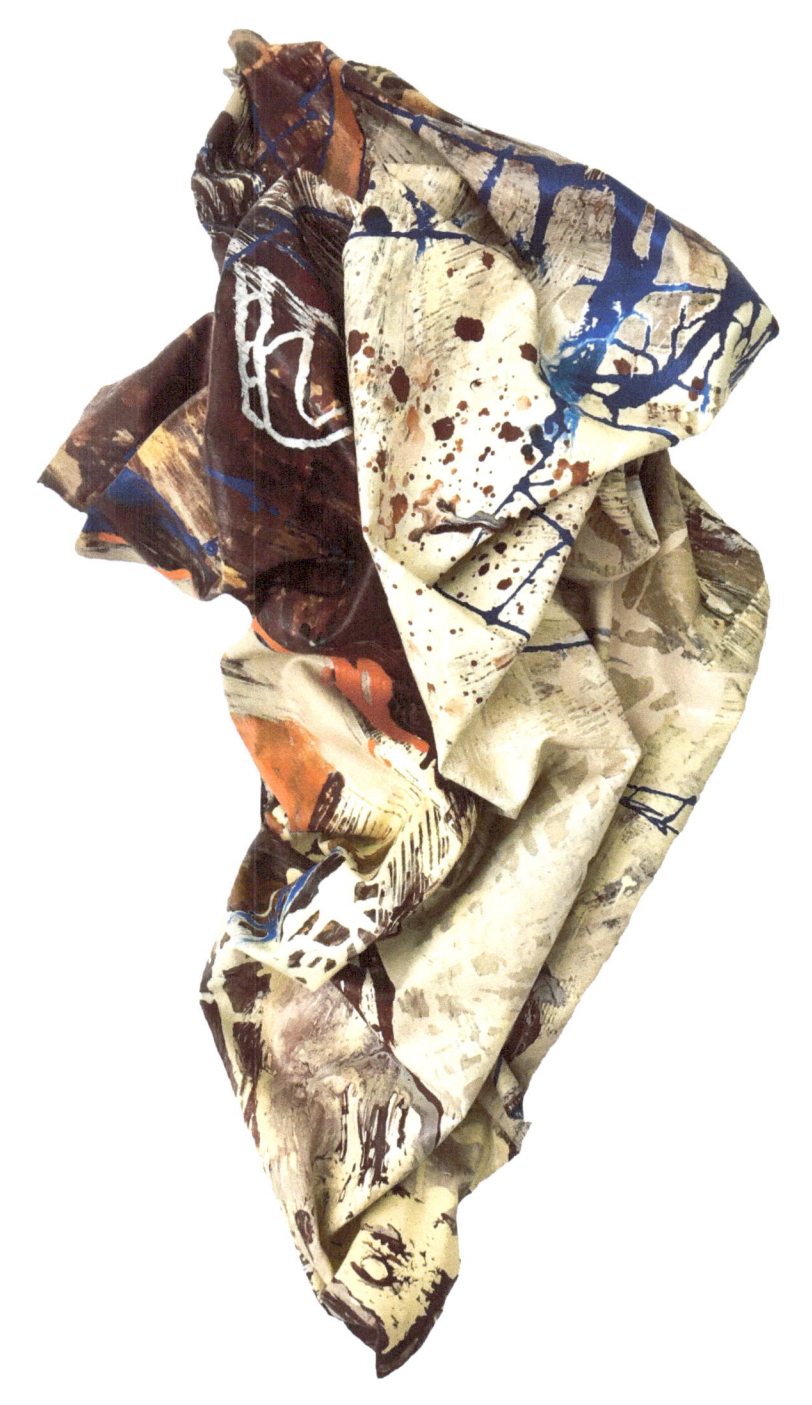

Striation Fan #2

acrylic on canvas
14"x28"x3"

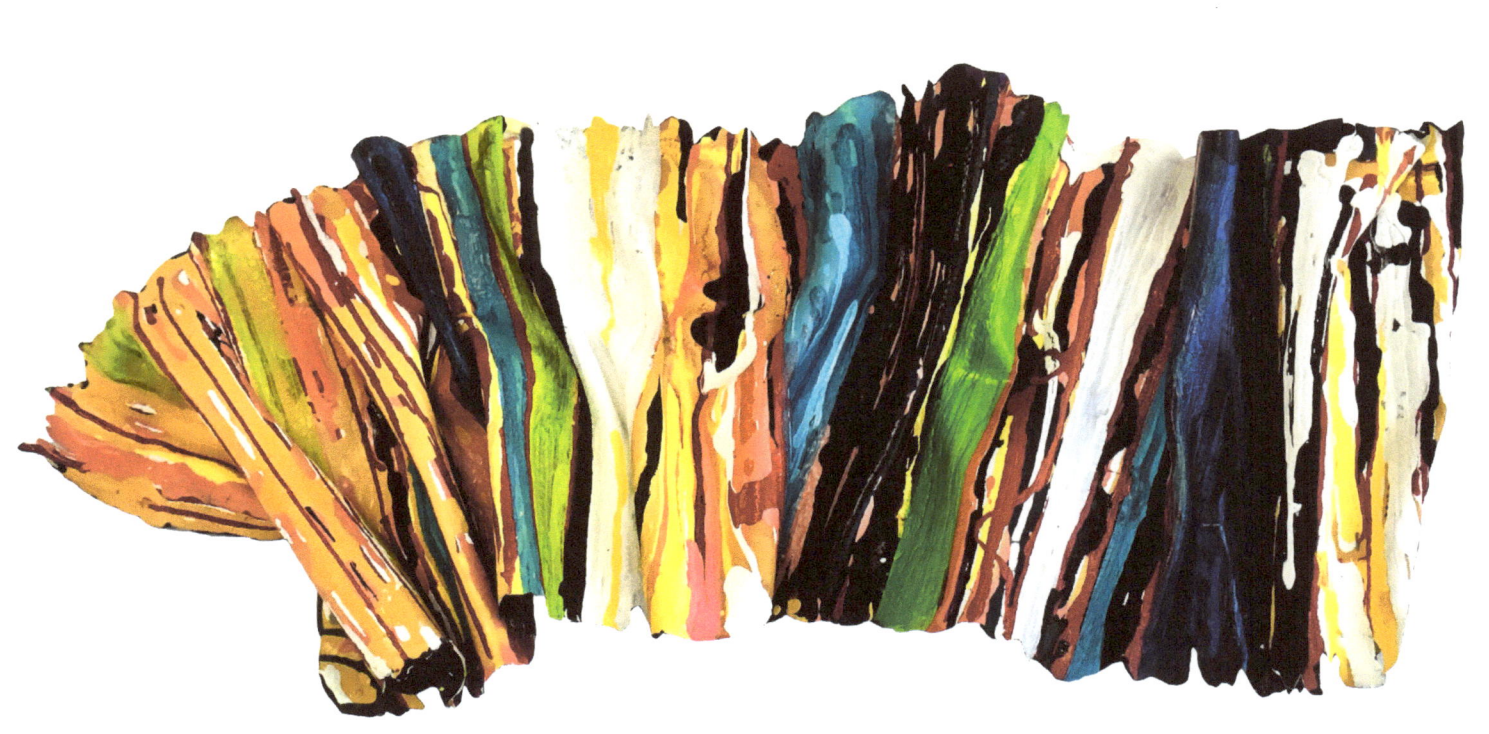

Untitled Map

acrylic on canvas
18"x36"x10"

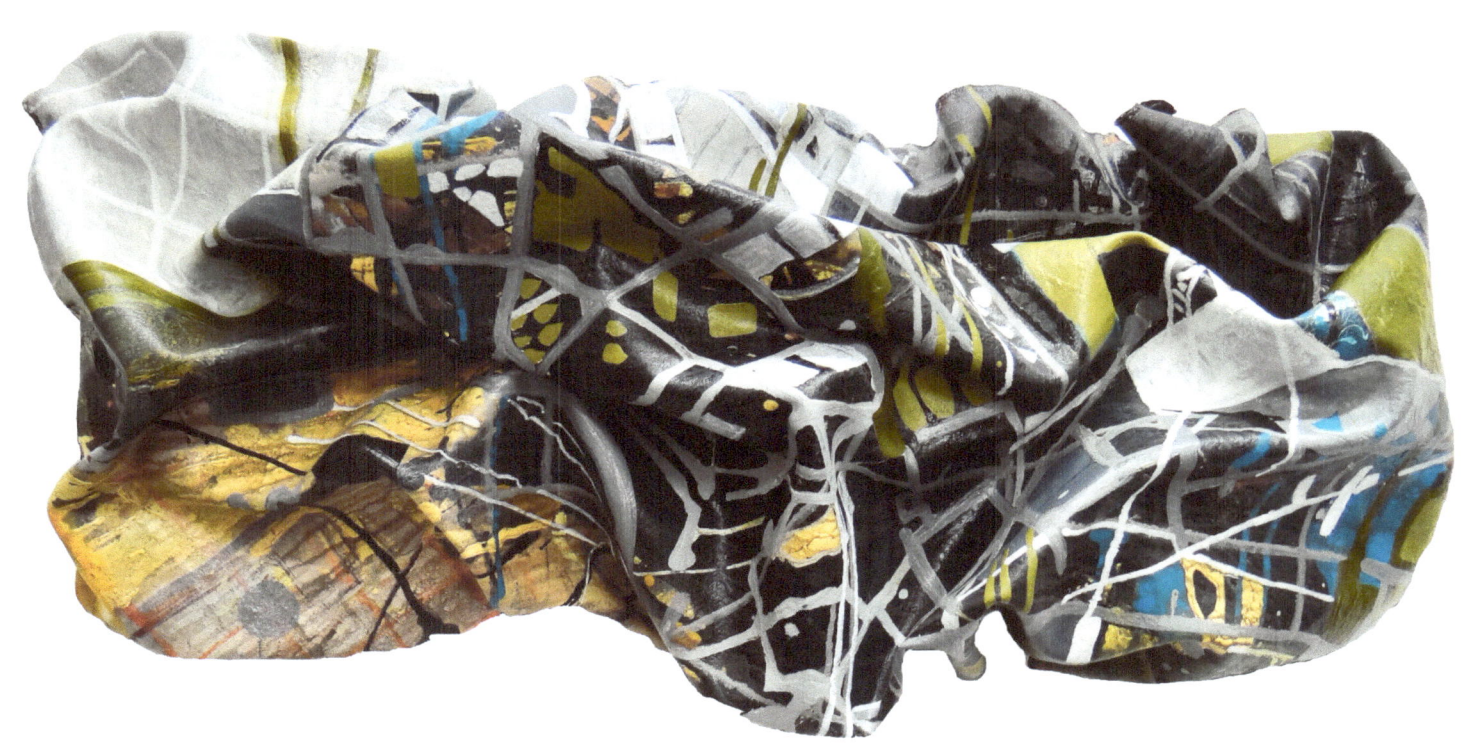

Maps of the Imagination

This series reflect my interest in maps, cartography, and topography. These paintings do not represent actual maps, but reference a composite collection of locations that intuitively evoke a sense of place. The paintings are constructed on the grid as an underlying structure of poured colored paints, richly layered surfaces that reveal and conceal strata and crust. I am interested in the physicality of landforms and the evidence of time and age as it emerges from the residue of human marks.

No Boots on the Ground

acrylic on canvas
36"x48"

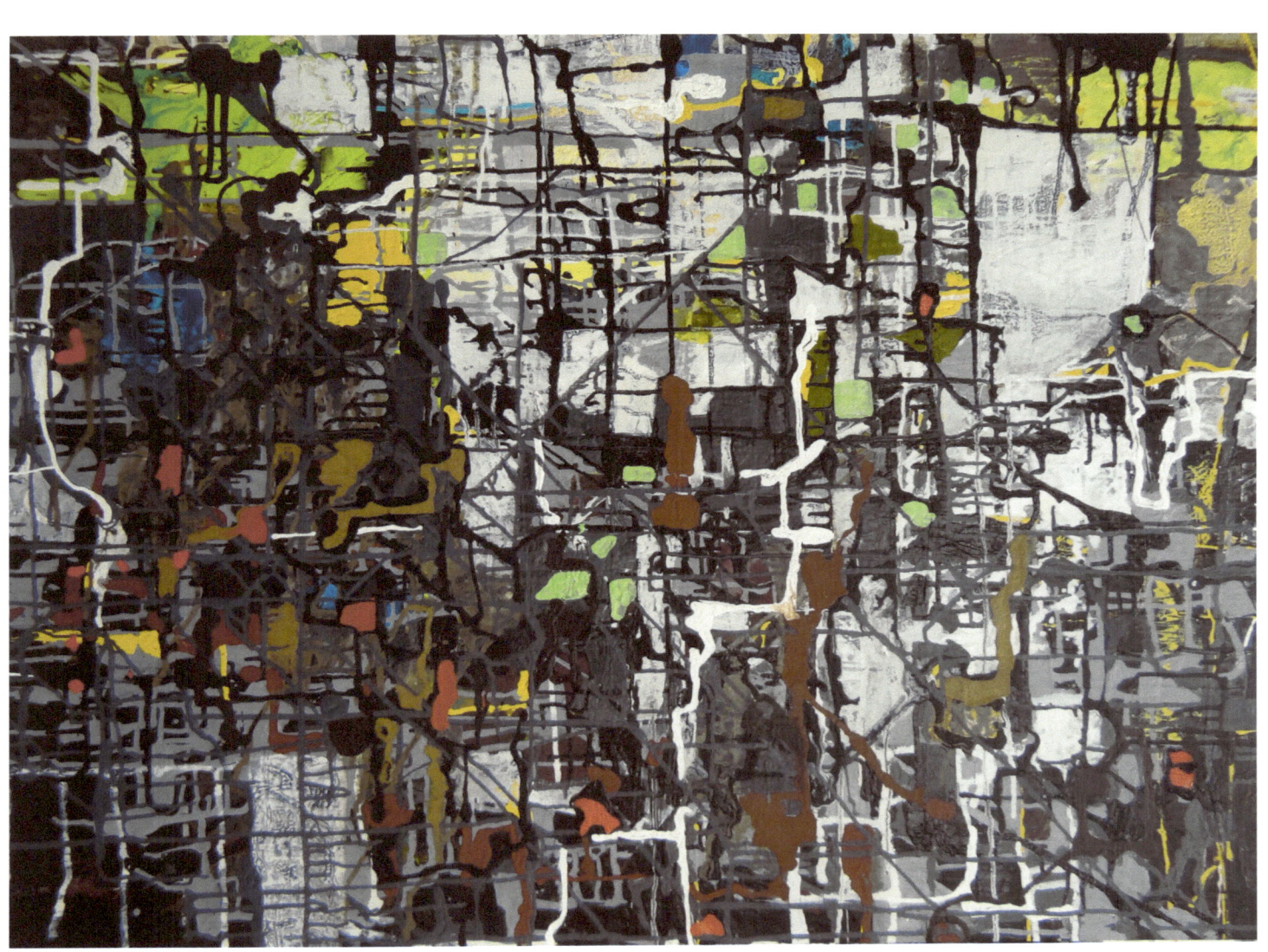

Polar Vortex

acrylic on canvas
48"x60"

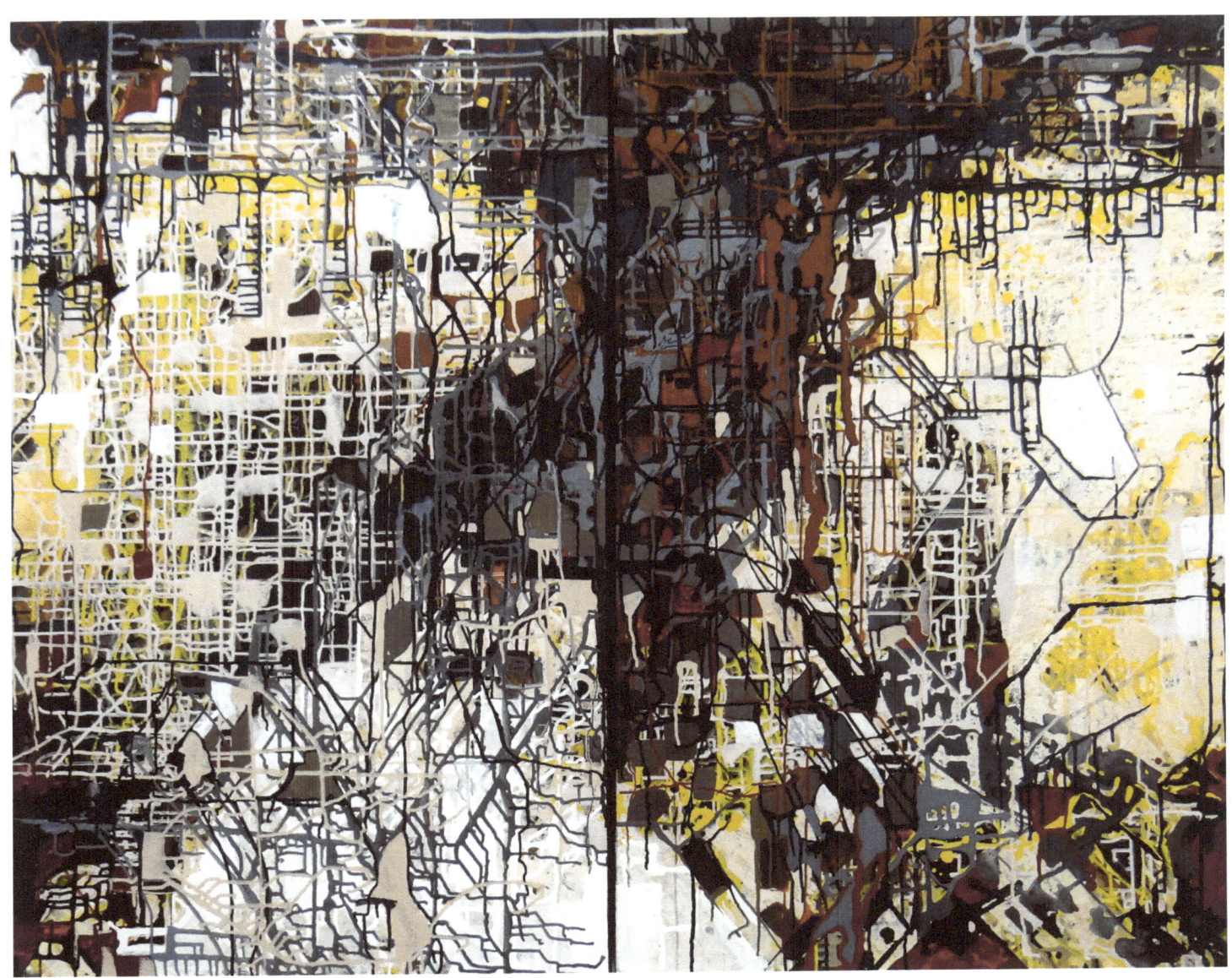

Excavating Pompeii

acrylic on paper
30"x50"

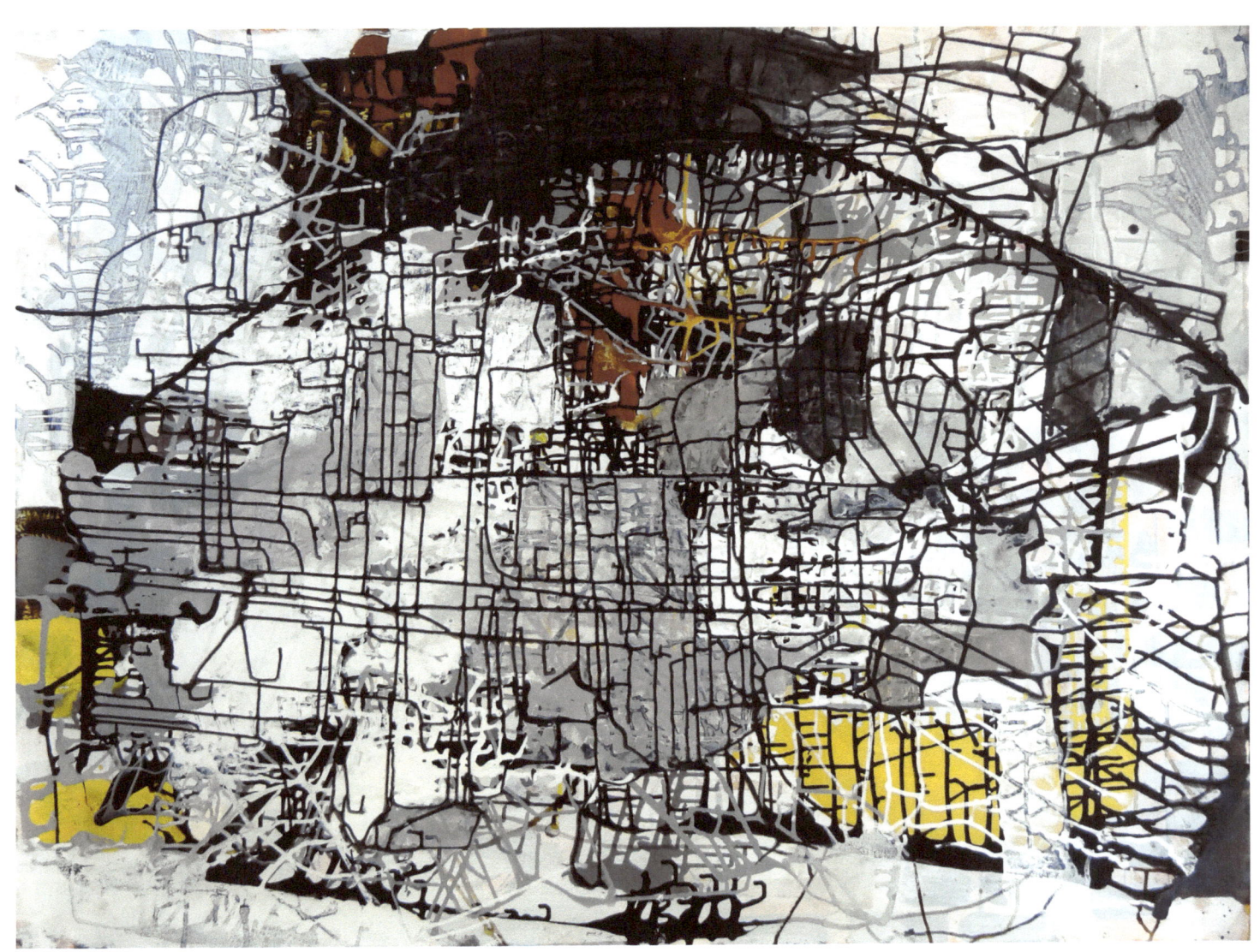

The Odyssey

acrylic on canvas
42"x54"

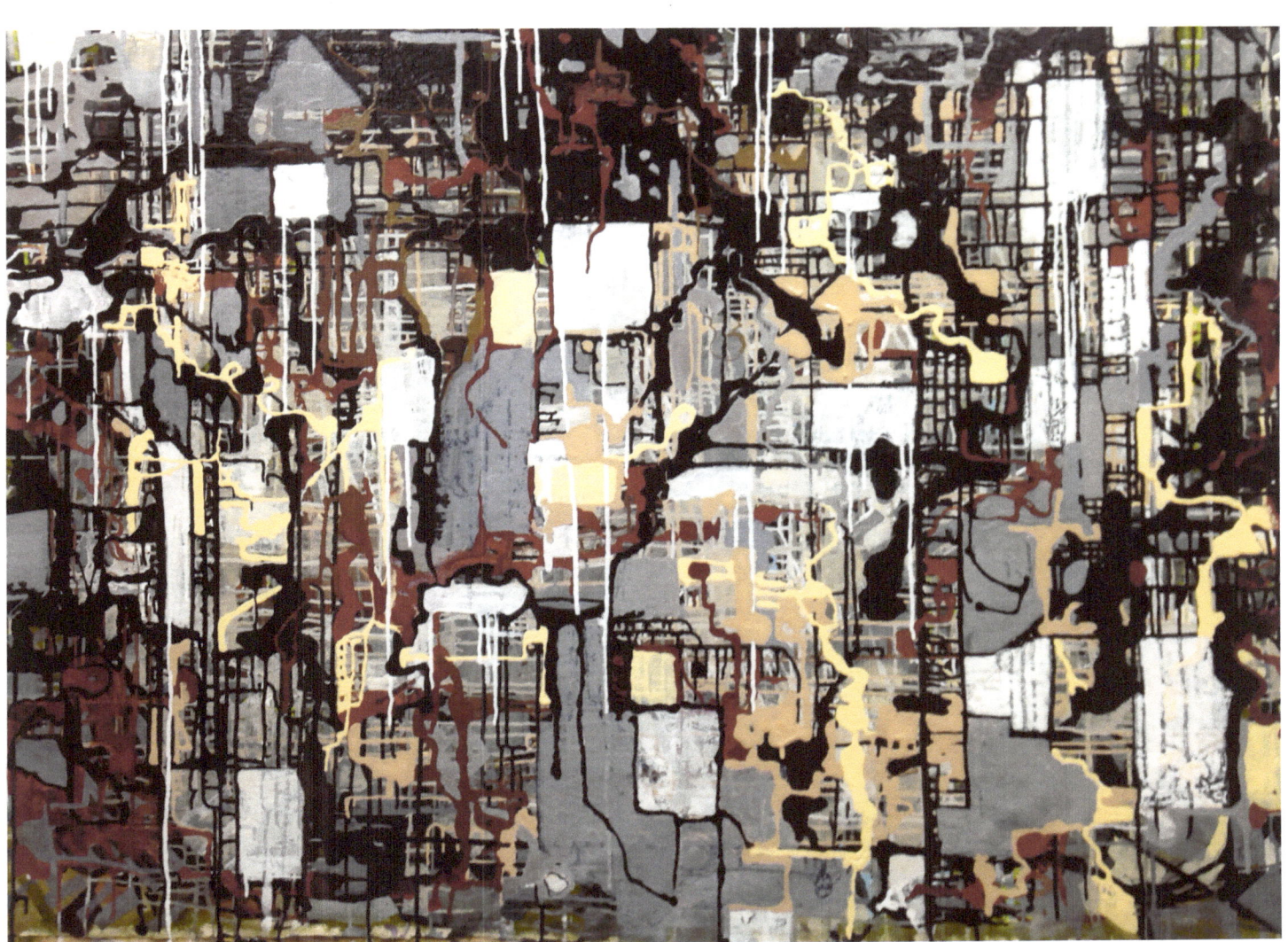

Isolated

acrylic on canvas
48"x36"

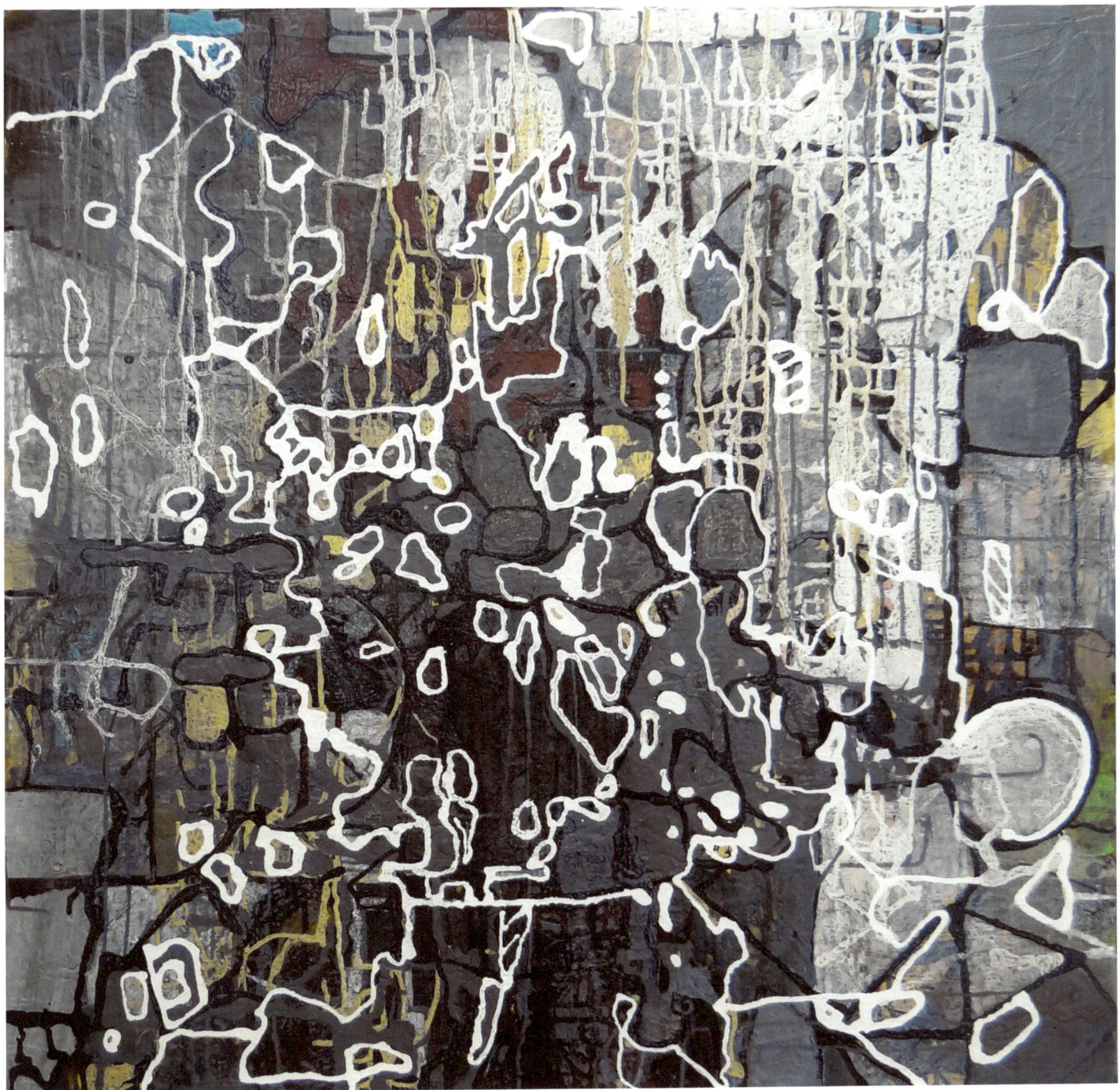

Sangre Tierra

acrylic on canvas
42"x50"

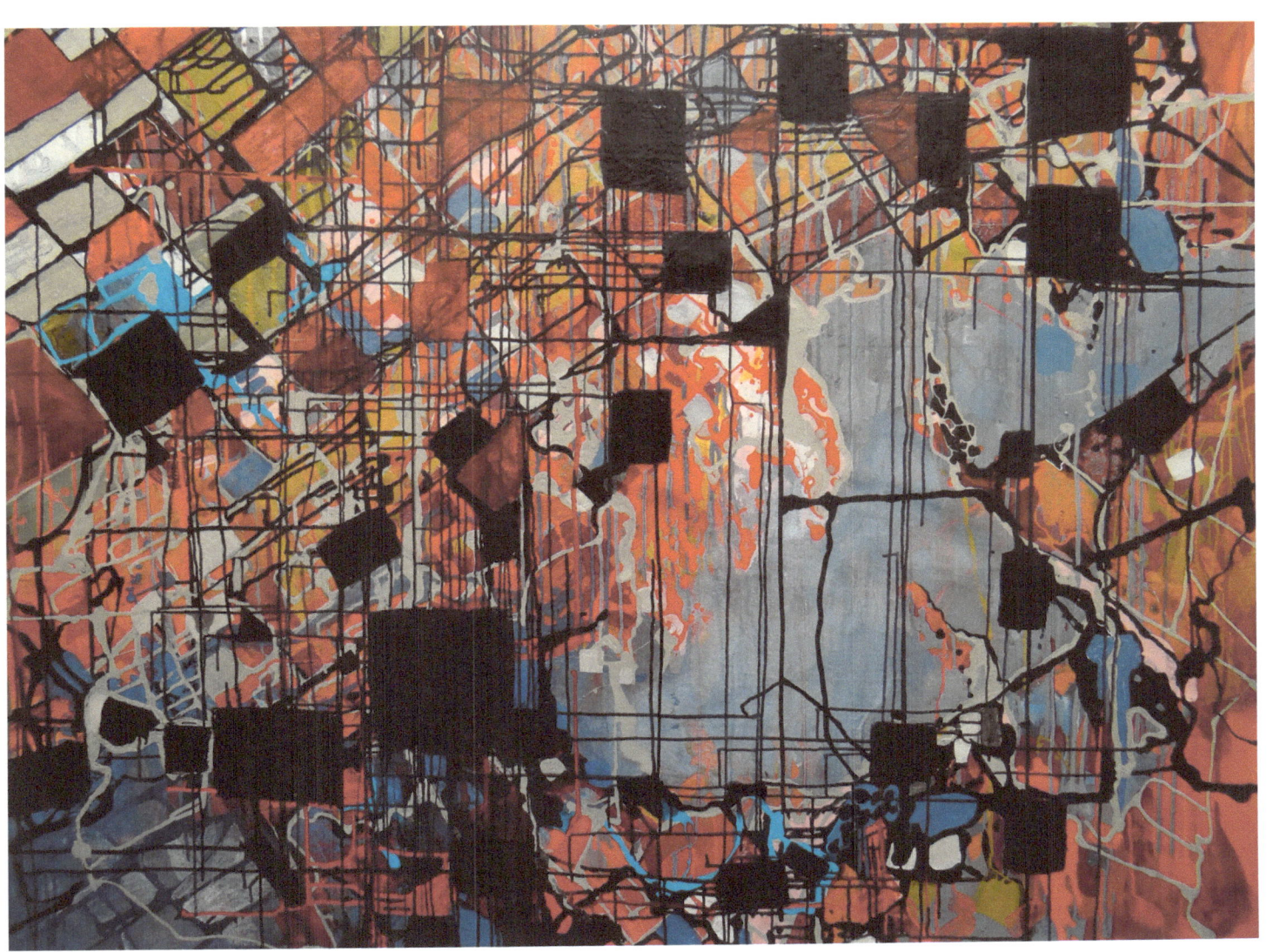

Winter Series #6

acrylic on paper
30"x42"

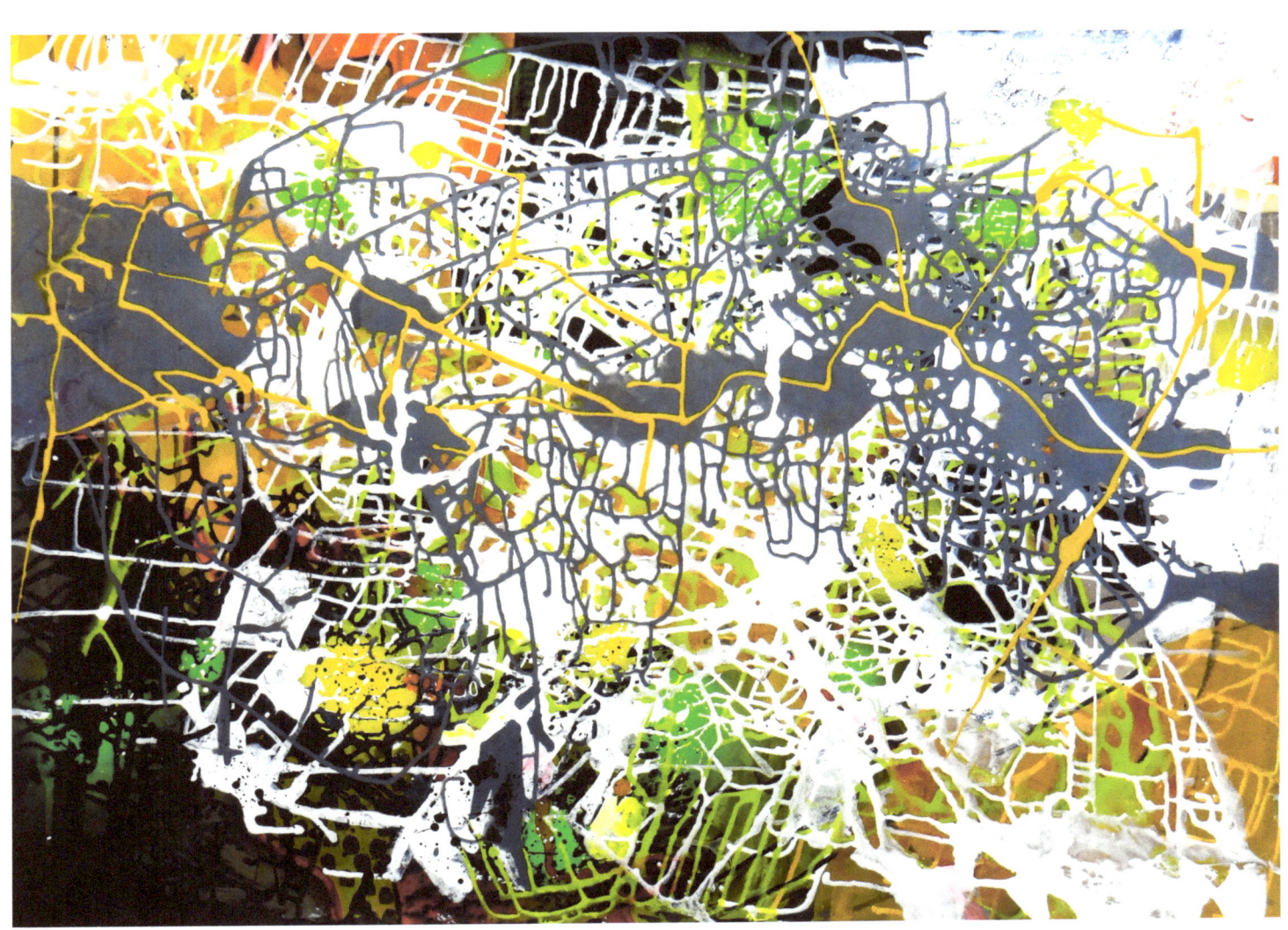

Winter Series #8

acrylic on paper
30"x42"

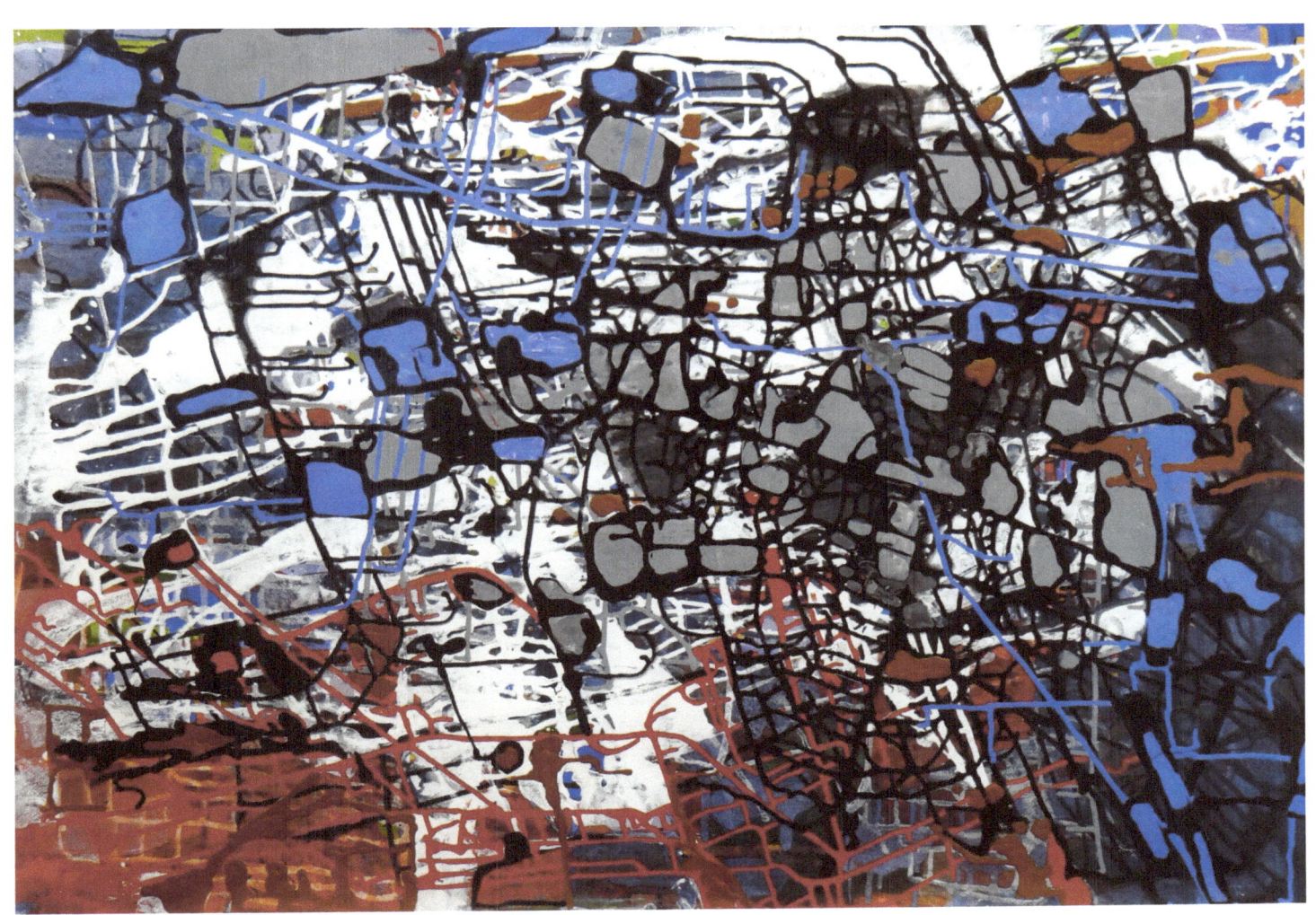

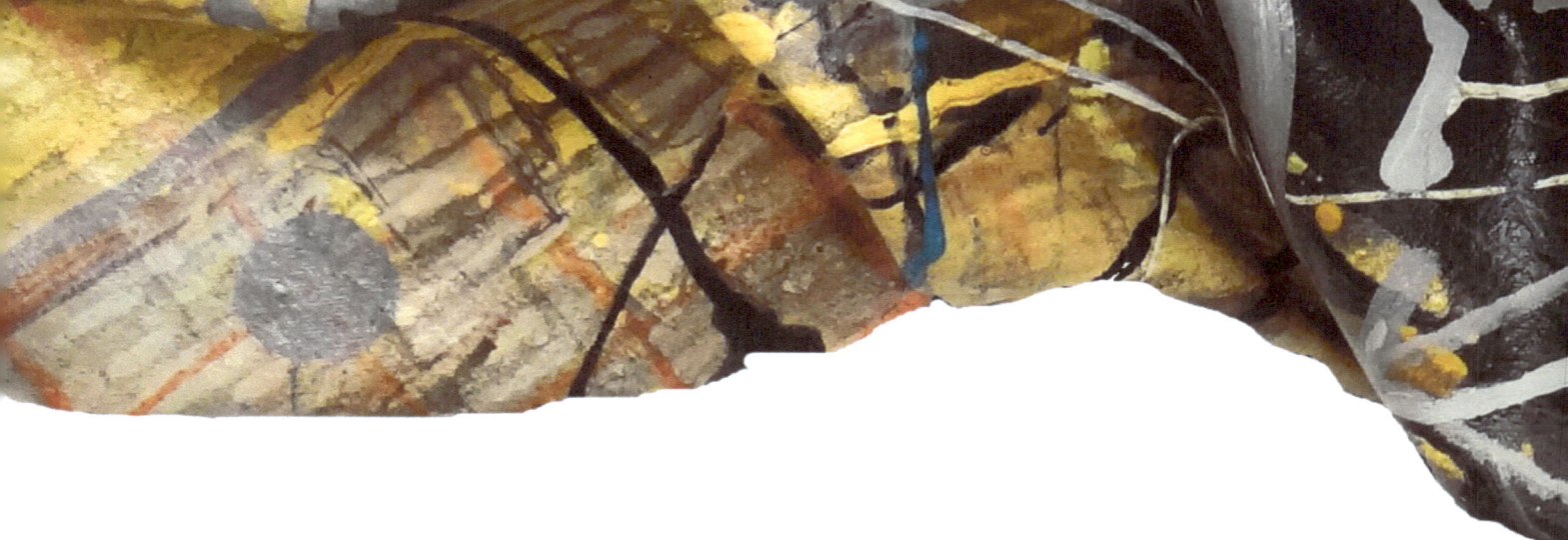

Bio

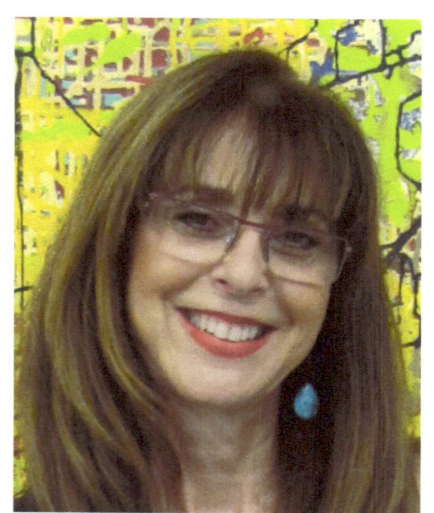

Shelley Heffler was born and raised in the Bronx. She attended the Fashion Institute of Technology in New York where she studied interior design, followed by a Bachelor's Degree in Art. She graduated from Cal State Northridge with a Master's degree in fine art followed by a teaching credential. She traveled extensively throughout Europe and Asia photographing the lives of fascinating people and the rich cultural landscape they live in. On returning from her travels, she settled in Los Angeles where she taught ceramics and fine art for L.A. Unified for over 25 years. Additionally, she was an adjunct professor at Otis College of Art and Design, a Nationally Board Certified Professional Educator, and a mentor teacher. Her exhibition history includes the Los Angeles County Museum of Art rental gallery, the Los Angeles Municipal Art Gallery and group shows throughout the United States. Her work has been reviewed in the British magazine Hedge, Los Angeles Times, LA Independent, Daily News, San Diego Tribune and San Diego Art Review. She was nominated for the Awards for the Visual arts, and received a Fellowship from Funds for Teachers. Her paintings and photographs are in the collections

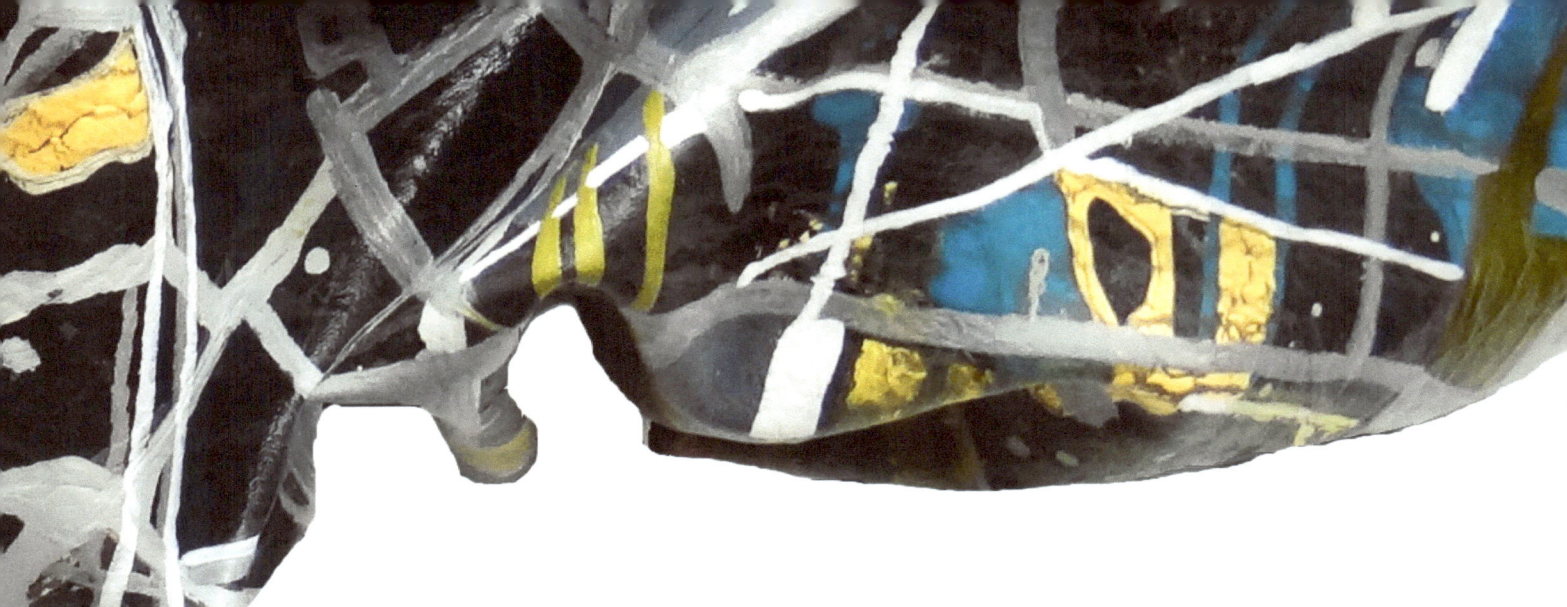

of many collectors across the United States. She has recently been identified as "One to Watch" on Saatchi On Line, and featured in "Art Pins". Now retired from teaching, she is solely dedicated to her art practice in her studio located at Beacon Arts in Inglewood, California.

Heffler's flourishing art practice is informed by a passion for maps which began as a young girl navigating the subways of NYC. Always viewing the world with wonder, she created an internal dialogue of her thoughts and feelings which made their way to an artistic voice. Primarily a painter who continues to be inspired by cartography as well as digital imagery from NASA, topography, and a deep concern for the interconnectedness of the world in terms of human values and experiences. Often, using a thick application of acrylic paint she covers her canvases with gestural brushwork creating richly layered surfaces that conceal and reveal the underlying history of paint application. The urge to morph some of her canvases into sculptural forms has a connection to pushing the boundaries of what is considered painting. There is always a question, what if? Many of her works are anthropocenic and focus on the shifting boundaries of land. In her words, "I create hybrid paintings confronting the unsettling engagement of human alterations to land and earth. I am inspired by science and ecological systems that represents an interconnectedness in the world we share."

www.ingramcontent.com/pod-product-compliance
Lightning Source LLC
Chambersburg PA
CBHW051051180526
45172CB00002B/600